Prayer is a Hunger

Titles in the *Prayer and Practice* Series

Prayer is a Hunger

Edward J. Farrell

Sheed and Ward · London

Contents

Foreword

Prayer tomorrow begins today or there will be no prayer tomorrow. The penalty of not praying is the loss of one's capacity to pray! The promise of tomorrow is the hunger of today. As man reaches out to the stars and touches ever expanding space, he is drawn to the discovery and value of his inner space. Prayer no longer lies on the edge of life. It moves into the core of the person's life and meaning. Without prayer, there is no way, no truth, no life.

Prayer becomes presence and reverence, reverence with others in community. Fraternity is a depth dimension of community, beyond group dynamics. Fraternity with Jesus is the source of authentic Christian life and community.

Prayer is a journey, a path that is created only by walking it. It creates and reveals oneself in the process. There are many ways of prayer, some new, some to be rediscovered. Writing is a way of discovering one's own gift of prayer. Scripture, Penance and Eucharist are Christ's way of praying in us. Discovering His gifts is to discover Him and those closest to Him. Eventually one is led out to the desert where one discovers the new creation and becomes a new creature.

1   Prayer Is A Hunger

St. Ignatius, on one of his journeys with his followers, had hired a porter to carry their bags. Periodically, the group stopped and prayed together. As the porter watched them, he wondered what they were doing; and, as the days went by, he began to want to do what they were doing. Ignatius, when the porter's desire became known to him, realized that this humble man was, through his desire to pray, praying the finest prayer of them all.

Prayer for many of us has become an enigma. It is difficult even to talk about it since nothing is more personal than one's prayer life. Each person *is* his prayer. When one thinks about prayer, he thinks of his own experience of it rather than of what prayer is. When he talks to someone else he is talking to someone whose experience is also an individual experience. A contributing factor to our difficulty is the nature of our times.

So much has happened to us in this particular era to make us think more profoundly about many areas of experience including, and perhaps especially, prayer. In a spiritual sense, it is as though we have gone through a sound barrier. We find ourselves thinking in ways people have never thought before. Or it may be that more people are thinking than have ever thought before. We are experiencing not only a pluralistic society, but each of us is also experiencing himself as a pluralistic person. Each of us can say that our name is Legion, that we contain, or feel that we contain, many different personalities within ourselves.

Through the communications explosion, we are open to much which was never before available. Such a proliferation of experiences has had an effect on us not only as learning creatures but also as believers. We find ourselves asking questions which we never before asked; we find ourselves experiencing realities which we had never before experienced. All of this makes new demands on us.

It asks of us, for example, a new dimension of faith, a deeper prayer; yes, and that we even be another kind of person. We are surrounded by extraordinary possibilities and extraordinary graces for us, for the Church, for all mankind. We are, as it were, in ascension, moving towards new heights. No longer within a particular small culture, a provincial culture, perhaps a ghetto culture, we have become citizens not only of a country but of the world; citizens, indeed, of the cosmos.

This rapid change, the expanding dimensions, has shaken us into creating new patterns, intellectual and spiritual. The emergence of the young into a powerful group has been for the good of all, if at times a rather shattering experience.

Students today take things more seriously than most of us took them; in school or even in the seminary. They ask questions. They ask about prayer, for prayer is to them of serious concern. They ask pragmatic questions: "Does prayer work? Is it meaningful? Does it make a difference? Is it making a difference?" These are valid questions. Each one of us might profitably ask himself, "Is prayer making a difference in my life; and what is that difference?"

We must consider, therefore, "What can prayer do? What is prayer itself?" The kinds of prayer to which we have been exposed have, for most people, become inadequate. We have come to realize that meaningful prayer is not an action, not a habit, not an impulse. Rather, it is fundamentally a person in relationship to another Person. Prayer is ourself, even as we are our grace.

Most of us are amateurs—those who love; and, in terms of prayer, who seek, desire, strive, are drawn to it. Prayer should be the most significant fact of our lives, because it is our selves that are involved. As grace is effected in us only because of personal relationship—we are our grace—so also is prayer effected in us because of our person to Person relationship.

The most frequent frustration which one hears from people is that although they want to pray, and they try to pray, they do not feel that they pray at all. Their prayer, if anything, they feel, seems to diminish. Part of the problem lies in the images we have of prayer, our expectations, the myths we have concerning it. Prayer is many faceted. It must be related to the fundamental reality of what truth does, of what Love does, of what happens when we are in the presence of someone.

Prayer is like a journey, a journey which we can never cease making. It is like thinking, for each day a man thinks again, never knowing when he may turn a corner in his thought and find himself in a world he had never perceived before. Each day a man loves, but he never loves today exactly as he did yesterday nor will he love tomorrow in the same way as he loved today.

Prayer is, in another dimension, always a mystery of person; and what it is to be a person is forever a mystery. What is it to be a creature who thinks, a creature who loves, and a creature who is willing to be with someone?

When we talk of prayer, when we talk of person, we are immediately involved in interiority, in inter-subjectivity, in inter-presence. It is intensely involving, once we begin to experience the awe, the wonder, the mystery in our relationships to people. And there is, in prayer, the presence of Christ, the presence which we believe and affirm: the presence of Christ in sacrament; the presence of Christ in people; the presences of Christ which are, in some way, so unsettling to people today. How do we pray? It depends upon the framework we give to prayer. St. Paul says, "Whatever you do in word or in work, do to the honor and and glory of God." Everything *can* be a prayer, in this sense, but that is a kind of prayer which leaves no room for what may be called "pure prayer."

There is a prayer which we can experience through nature, a kind of pre-evangelical prayer, the prayer of all men. We may have this kind of prayer in the tender presence of the beauty of nature. The sun, the grass, the architectural beauty of the earth creates in us a "Thank You," in a simple spontaneous prayer which arises involuntarily. It is a valid prayer. It is one of the sacraments of God in a small letter; but all the world is a word to us, a communication. "God so loved the world" that He became incarnate in its beauty, and made us in such a way that we express Him when we rejoice and celebrate His creation. It is real prayer, a prayer which we are in more than we realize.

There is, also, the prayer which we can experience with another person; in a real meeting of Christ in another person if we contemplate the meaning and significance of the sacraments. The authentic presence of Christ is not only in the Eucharist. Christ is indeed present in the Eucharist, on the altar, and in the tabernacle, under the form of bread—which is a sign, which is intended to be united with a human person. The deepest presence of Christ is in the Incarnational reality of this union, this personal union which is the most real presence of Christ in us.

Christ is the first sacrament, the primal sacrament; and each one of us, in the reality that we are Christ, is this presence to one another, because faith comes only through people, only through persons. This is a reality which we are only dimly beginning to perceive—an extraordinary reality. Christ comes to us in His Word, in Scripture, in the active word of the sacrament; and something happens to us. The love of Christ changes us. We are different as persons because Christ really affects us as persons. We are constantly and continually being formed. St. Paul says, "You are a new creature in Christ." And we are new. It is an almost overwhelming reality. It is a psychological reality, not only an ontological reality, not only in terms of essence and being, but existentially.

All of this is not only a reality, it is a mystery; that Christ does communicate himself to us as persons, and thereby gives us the capacity to communicate ourselves to others in a more complete way. Christ's relationship to us, to all men, creates, one might say, fields or currents, fields which ripple with activity so that we can have a radiation effect upon others and they a radiant effect upon us. It is as if there were generated "person energy." Perhaps the only adequate way we can try to explain what happens between people is that we energize each other. As Christ energizes us, and we energize others, it becomes a reciprocal never-ending, intensifying reality. All of us are members of Christ. Unamuno once said "your neighbor is your unknown self." Each time we meet another person we discover something about ourselves which we did not know before because we have discovered something of that person.

The new theology, which suggests that in some way there is only one man, is saying what St. Augustine said many centuries ago, "And there shall be one Christ loving Himself." The interpretation of which we are capable results from this mystery of Christ. Paul and Peter spoke of ministering to each other the grace that was within them. We, too, are to minister grace to one another. We are to activate the Christ that is in each of us. This is a great mystery of Christian community. There is in it a unique presence which cannot be replaced by anything else. This communication is a kind of prayer.

But there is a unique community with Christ Himself which is different from the prayer of nature, different from the communication between human persons. It is a communication which we can have with Christ alone; which no other person, no other love, no other truth, no other knowledge can ever give. Today it would seem that our prayer is coming into consciousness of this relationship and of the capacity we have for it.

We have sometimes become so enthralled, so absorbed by our capacity to relate to other people that it can involve all our attention. We can then say truly, "I have hardly any time left for Christ. I have hardly any time left for prayer." The enjoyment and exuberance which follows our experience of another person can even make us think, "What need do I have for God if I can be so fulfilled by my relationships with people?" This may be a necessary stage in growth. It is a real kind of prayer. But it is not enough.

If we were to stop at this stage we would be missing the real advent of Christ, the real presence of Christ, and missing the most important reality for ourselves. Christ is an Absolute to us. Everything else is relative to that Absolute. Prayer is a relationship; it is not an entity in itself. It is a relationship to Christ. We must recognize that Christ is not a Person as other persons. We need a new vocabulary to talk about relationship to Christ; it is not the same as interpersonal relationships to people, and it cannot be equated with it.

When we speak of Christ we speak of Him in Whom we "live, move, and have our being," out of Whom, and in Whose image we were formed, Who is our finality. We have a destiny. All of us can experience this sense of destiny. We have, each of us, within ourselves the love that has not been expressed, the truth which has not been understood, the potentiality which has not been actualized. We are moving towards what we do not fully understand. We experience this movement within us.

Prayer, then, is essentially a mystery because Christ is a mystery. Because we are in His image, we too are a mystery. We still do not know who we are. Yet we know that Christ calls us to pray, to enter into relationship, into personal union with Him, a union rivalled only by the hypostatic union. It is the call of Christ to know Him. And to the degree that we know Him, we begin to know who we are, and to know one another. It is by loving God that we come to love men; and by loving men we come to love God.

Prayer is also a work, a discipline. It cannot rest upon mere spontaneity. It does not come easily, just as being a person does not come easily. And prayer is the greatest, highest expression of us as persons. We will pray in the measure that we come to be persons; and we come to be persons in the measure that we pray. If one is a person, he is in contact with the landscape of reality; and Christ is the greatest Reality of the landscape.

Prayer means also an entering into timelessness. One of the beautiful expressions of contemporary philosophy included in the Pope's document of the Development of People is that "Man infinitely transcends himself." Prayer is the key to the transcendence of man, even its essential key. It is a becoming. It is our uncompleted task, our uncompleted task of becoming ourselves; our uncompleted journey. Prayer is a waiting. It is hunger; it is love. Prayer is a relatedness, and prayer is a stillness.

What do we need to learn in order to pray? We must learn a new dimension in communicating. Moreover, we must learn that a primary dimension of Christian prayer is receiving, is learning to listen. Listening is rare. There are certain people we meet to whom we feel we can talk because they have such a deep capacity for hearing; not hearing words only but hearing us as a person. They enable us to talk on a level which we have never before reached. They enable us to *be* as we have never been before. We shall never truly know ourselves unless we find people who can listen, who can enable us to emerge, to come out of ourselves, to discover who we are. We cannot discover ourselves by ourselves.

In prayer before Christ we must listen even as we are listened to. It takes time. We should have a place of prayer. Each of us needs not only a temple, not only a church, but also a holy place, holy because of the experience that has come to us in this place. And we should return often to our holy place.

Someone once asked a friend, "How do you teach someone to pray?" She paused for a moment, then answered, "You cannot teach prayer. He must find someone who prays and he will learn from that person."

Our Lord's authority lay in His capacity to create in others the desire to be like Him. He gave them also the capacity to be what they could be. This is an awesome responsibility that we, too, have: to *be* in such a way that others will desire what we have spiritually. And who of us dares to speak like St. Paul, "Be you imitators of me as I am of Christ. Do what I am doing." Yet this is what is demanded, and young people today are demanding that we be credible; that we be what we say. They cannot take the message unless we are the medium. And they know it well. We must be the medium. This is why we must pray.

Prayer, as we have said, is a stillness. There is, also, a decision required, for prayer is the easiest habit to be unaccustomed to. A small motto states, "Now is the great beginning." How true it is. Every day, prayer has to be begun again. Being a person, being someone who loves, who understands and listens, bends to the unfinished task—each day a beginning, a "now." Prayer is a risk. If we really pray, we never know what is going to be asked of us. It is a dangerous thing to pray if we take it seriously.

Prayer is a growing; it is a discovering; it is a communion, a communion most of all with Him in whom all things are. Prayer is an inscape, the totality of the universe experienced in the minutest atom.

One barrier to real prayer is a lack of courage, a lack of perseverance. Why do we often choose so low a ceiling? There is nothing sadder than to "settle" in one place; to build walls, to travel no longer on the Abrahamic journey. It is perilously easy for us to be no longer on our way to Jerusalem. Yet we must go on this journey.

If only we could believe the truth, the magnificent process in which we are, the discovery of the reality in Christianity, the reality which we already have and to which we are not adequately sensitive—then something would happen. If we believe the truth that Christ as a Person is continually incarnating Himself in our life; and that through every Mass Christ really unites Himself to us, then we will expand and grow in His greatness. We will be given new eyes, new ears, we will be given a new heart, a new mind; and this will happen continuously in Christ. We may speak of it as always being aware that we are becoming "pregnant" with the reality of Christ; that at any moment the capacities within ourselves will be actualized. St. Paul spoke of "being in labor until Christ is formed in us." The reality of Christ's being present to us and in us transforming us, changing us: this should be for us a constant awareness, a constant thanksgiving. Prayer, rightly understood, is an expression of the deepest levels of our being. The beginning of prayer is need. On a human interpretation, there is perhaps no justification for prayer; no reason for prayer in itself. If one wants to think of it as a tranquilizer, a kind of straightening up of one's mind, he may do that; but that is not prayer. Prayer for the Christian is always a response to the living Christ, to the living Person. Anything less than that is inadequate. It must be the living Presence of Christ.

If one's prayer is on this deep level, he will understand the mystery of grace and the mystery of prayer—that it is beautiful, that it attracts, that it draws as Christ drew people to Him. There was only one question which Christ asked Peter even when Peter had failed again and again, "Do you love me?" Can we say that we love Christ if there is not an intimate, ongoing, day-by-day relationship with Him? It is only through this power of Christ within ourselves that we can draw, and change, and renew.

Prayer will, if seriously undertaken, create a tension in our life, a struggle for balance. There will be the incarnational tension expressed by the Cross which is rooted in the earth yet stretches to the sky. There is pure prayer, yet there is total action, and no one ever reaches a final equilibrium. There is always the need that we open ourselves to life, to the world, and to God. Prayer will, despite the struggle (perhaps because of it) give us some unity and continuity to our life. It will be open to the transcendence that is there. Contemplation must be the goal of all our lives because God *is* the *end* and peak of it, and that end and peak must be contained in some way in every action of our life. There must be the realization that the Kingdom of God has already begun.

When Christ is in our presence, we might say that the whole body of Christ is present to us. The saints are in our lives, they are not at a distance. There are so many and varied and wonderful ways of praying. We cannot pray in a vacuum. We cannot have a conversation with God that is not real; and a basic way of prayer is reading from the Scripture. Christ speaks to us through His Word, ongoing and continuous. Christian prayer is always rooted in Scripture; energized through the sacraments.

There must be, also, a real rhythm in our life: some time every day, some extended prayer every week, and time each month for being "in the desert." This is an essential framework.

We shall not pray well, however, unless we become responsive to others in a visible, tangible way. The Christian experience is not an isolated experience; it is a relationship with others before God. There is something which happens in prayer when it is transformed into real love; not a love of the mind but an experiential and interpersonal perception of other people. We are intended to grow into this experience to realize in truth that the Body of Christ is not only a theological truth, but it is to be known and lived out by us. Through prayer, through this union with Christ, we shall discover and recognize this union in one another. It is then that we shall become truly catholic and Catholic.

When we speak of the prayer of contemplation, we think of experiencing the creative act of God ever continuing in us, filling us with being. To experience this is an adoration, a continuing adoration given us only through the gift of the Holy Spirit. Contemplation is the activity of the Holy Spirit in us.

There are, then, levels of prayer. There is the prayer in terms of creation. There is prayer in terms of interpersonal relationships. And there is the distinctive Christian level of prayer which is only from and in the Spirit. We are trying in our age to discover and to recognize what this mysterious activity of the Holy Spirit in us is, enabling us to pray, to move to the deepest levels of spiritual intensity. Martin Luther King once said, "I have been to the mountain." We must go up to Jerusalem, to the mountain of prayer, the mountain of contemplation, the mountain of adoration.

If we truly pray, we shall be continually attaining toward the prayer of abandonment: "Father, I abandon myself in Your hands. Do with me what You will. Whatever You may do, I thank You. I am ready for all; I accept all. Let Your will be done in me and in all Your creatures. I wish no more than this, O Lord. Into Your hands I commend my spirit. I offer to You all the love of my heart, for I love You, Lord, and I give myself, surrender myself into Your hands without reserve, with boundless confidence, for You are my Father."

2   The Journal
A Way Into Prayer

If the lost word is lost, if the spent word is spent
If the unheard, unspoken
Word is unspoken, unheard;
Still is the unspoken word, the Word unheard,
The Word without a word, the Word within
the world and for the world;
and the light shone in darkness and
against the Word the unstilled world still whirled
about the centre of the silent Word

Ash Wednesday–
T.S.Eliot

Prayer is a hunger, a hunger that is not easily quieted. Today the cry "teach us to pray" echoes and reverberates from many directions. One of the ways I have learned to pray is by writing. I began by copying favorite passages from reading, then thoughts and ideas of others and finally by jotting down my own insights and reflections from prayer and experiences of each day. This prayer journal at times seems like my own biography of Christ, a kind of Fifth Gospel. Writing makes me think of the Evangelists' experience. Why and how did Matthew, Mark, Luke and John begin their writing? What happened in them? What kind of grace was effecting them? Certainly their experience in writing was a prayer, an entering into the mind and heart of Christ. I wonder if the evangelist's experience is not to be a more common experience for many Christians.

God has expressed himself in a unique

and privileged way in Scripture, and yet He continues to reveal Himself and ourselves to us in the events of our everyday life. His written Word is fresh born each morning and he appeals to us "harden not your hearts this day as your fathers did in the desert" Ps 95. We dare to ask Him each day "Give us this day our daily bread," knowing that it is not by bread alone that man lives but by every word that comes from the mouth of God. The Father continues to communicate to each of us through the Spirit of His Son, "for the Spirit reaches the depths of everything, even the depths of God. After all the depths of a man can only be known by his own spirit, not by any other man and in the same way the depths of God can only be known by the Spirit of God. Now instead of the spirit of the world, we have received the Spirit that comes from God, to teach us to understand the gifts that he has given us." I Cor. 2, 10-12. Rahner somewhere writes "there are things which theologians try to explain. The Lord has other means of making them understood." Christ speaks to us each in a unique way. I think and pray and speak to him in a way no one else has ever spoken to Him. He speaks to me in a way that he has spoken to no one else. Moments of depth and rare insight, of meeting with God the sacred are to be treasured and pondered within the heart. What photography is to the visual, writing is to the intuitive and moment of light. Paul wrote, "If you read my words, you will have some ideas of the depths that I see in the mystery of Christ. (Eph. 34)

Writing enables us to see into the depths. It is not a simple recording of thoughts already finished but it is creative in its very activity and process. Writing is a journey, exploring the countries of the mind and heart, the never ending revelatory Word spoken once for all time. Little attention has been given to the value of writing as a way into prayer, an openness to contemplation, as a celebration and remembering, as discovery, as centering. Deep calls to deep and the deep conscious level responding to the deep not yet conscious reality of our being. In the beginning was the Word and it had to become incarnate.

There is I hope something of the Evangelist's grace for each of us, the grace of writing, of incarnating, infleshing the word in our self and imprinting it and making it our word. None of the Evangelists were "writers" in the professional sense, yet their writings were a deep communication with God, with themselves, with others. Our Lord frequently asked his listeners, "What do you think?" He constantly compels us to think, to contemplate! How sad it is that so often we lose our capacity for truth, for depth; numbness overloads our fuses and short circuits our perceptive faculties.

Writing creates an opening in the stream of unconsciousness and breaks up the automatic pattern of our life. One awakes to the newness that comes so unexpected each day. Our eyes see differently as through the wonder of a new camera. One becomes aware that this is the only moment like this that I shall ever have. The first conscious thought of the day becomes an exciting experience. As a person writes he begins to recognize an extraordinary relation between the hand as it writes and the mind and heart, like an ignition. What is written is not as significant as what happens to us in the process. Something is growing within; hidden capacity gently reveals itself. New sensitivities unfold. The horizon sweeps back, the veil lifts and we experience Emmaus, "did not our hearts burn within us as he talked to us and explained the scripture to us." Lu 24.32.

Rollo May describes creativity as "the encounter of the intensely conscious human being with his world." Writing is an experience of creativity immediately available to everyone. "To write one has but to begin, to take the risk, to take it seriously enough to play with it, for it is by walking that one creates the path." It is so easy to live outside of ourselves, to be unaware of the inner center, the inner dialogue, the inner journey. But once a man begins, he experiences the thrill of his own unique thoughts and insights. He begins to discern his own words from the borrowed words of others. What an acceleration to discover the "hidden manna" and He who gives him "a white stone, with a new name written on the stone which no one knows except him who receives it." Rev. 2:17. T. S. Eliot expresses it so simply:

"With the drawing of this Love and the
      Voice of this Calling
We shall not cease from exploration
And the end of all our exploring
Will be to arrive where he started
And know the place for the first time."

Writing is a way in to what is going on and developing within ourselves. It can become a powerful way of prayer, a key to self-understanding and inner dialogue. The power in writing stimulates the very inner process that it is engaged in describing, drawing the process further inward. It is not a passive retelling of events, or a describing of an experience. It becomes one's own experience. Nor is it a self-conscious analytical introspection. Expressing oneself in words is rather an active and continuing involvement in a personal inner process through which one is drawn into an expanded understanding of the reality in his own existence. For example, most people pray the Our Father every day. One can hear Christ's words and then suddenly hear. what his own heart is saying, "hallowed be my name, my kingdom come, my will be done." This inbreaking of understanding can become just another forgotten inspiration and lost grace or by getting it down it becomes specific, focused and decisive. If one writes regularly, no matter how briefly, a conscious thought, insight, prayer, reflection, he will find that it becomes a cumulative enrichment. It is tuning into what is going on, seeing the connection and relationship, capturing that which is behind the consciousness. Writing and contemplation tend to merge. We know the saints best who found themselves compelled to write—Augustine, Bernard, Catherine, Theresa and our own contemporaries John XXIII's *Journal of a Soul,* Dag Hammarskjold's *Markings.*

In this day of so much glib talk, when we are daily inundated and assaulted with unending words and speech, when everyone is correspondingly articulate on everything, the written personal word is increasingly important. Such words come out of silence and expand silence. They reestablish privacy so rare today, and a comfortable sense of solitude. They beget the dialogue between one's known self and one's deeper, unknown self that is coming into being. One begins to hear the wordless dialogue between one's deepest self and God. Christ taught his disciples through the deep questions—"Who do you say I am?" "Do you love me?" "What do you think?" We can not but respond to his questions and imperatives with our own questions and responses. "Is it I Lord?" "Where do you live?"

As never before each of us has to personalize our faith; we must initial it with our own name and make it ours. We must be able to give reason for the faith that is within us. People do not ask about the formal teachings of the Church. They want to know your experience, what you think, what difference does Jesus make? Here are some of the questions that I have been asked and that I write about in order that I may be ready to speak his word in me for others. "How do you pray?" "Who is Jesus for me?" "When do you believe?" "When do you love?" "How?" "When have you experienced penance?" "What difference does the Eucharist make in you?" "What do you expect of you?" "How does your vineyard grow?" "What is your charism?" "What is your sin?" "What would it take for you to be a saint now?" "What is Jesus asking of you today?" "What effect are you making on your world?" These questions demand thinking; they demand contemplation. Answering the questions in spoken words may avoid the implications of their personal meaning. Thinking is so diffused, unformulated, scattered, easily distracted. To write an answer for one's self is to drive deep; it disciplines, focuses and brings one to face Christ with his conviction.

A journal is a journey—the journey of today—both words are from the French word "le jour"—today. The journal is the coming into possession of life this day in the written word, capturing its secret, its mystery. The written word is perhaps more like a kiss than a possessing as in the words

of Blake:
He who bends to himself a joy
Doth the winged life destroy
But he who kisses the joy as it flies
Loves in Eternity's sunrise.

The journal calls for honesty, for a search into meaning. It is a discipline in a day when discipline is rare. "But it is a narrow gate and a hard road that leads to life, and only a few find it" Mt. 7, 14. Time set aside to move from the outer to the inner, to discover new depths, to see new connections, to perceive fresh insight— surely this work is prayer. It is at times unselfconscious poetry and contemporary psalmody. The journal is a putting into words the praise of God that leaps from the transparencies of life which the light of faith illumines for us. Each of us has our own unique psalms, the journal helps us to find the words which in turn we share with those he sends to us. Each must honor the desire to express oneself or not. Every person has his own inner rhythm and each must have his own way of getting to it.

Writing Together

When people come together and are silent, something in addition becomes present. "Where two or three are gathered together in my name, there am I in the midst of them." Mt. 18, 20. As a group turns their focus from outside to inside, to a level of depth, something else becomes present and makes other kinds of experiences possible. This contact with ourselves would not happen by oneself. A cumulative atmosphere of depth allows us to come to new depth within ourselves. One of the more fruitful group prayer experiences that I have worked with is using a three hour block of time. A group of six to ten sit in a small circle in the presence of the Eucharist or with the open Scripture and lighted candles, in the center. The first hour is a prayer of adoration, of silent witness to the Presence in the presence of each other. This hour is an experience of silence and hiddenness with the Father. "You are dead and your life is hidden with Christ in God." The second hour is the hour of writing—the quantum leaps from nothingness into creation—the power of a word pulling many things into understanding. Out of the silence the word comes forth. A field of energy is generated by the concentration of the others around oneself and one is supported by the current of their efforts. The hour of writing is more than a remembering the hour in silence. It is an unfolding experience in itself that carries new dimensions of perception with it. The third hour is one of sharing, of speaking the word to one another. The sharing is at a depth level because of the common experience of the previous two hours—it is no longer an exchange of words and ideas, it is a meeting of persons. In some dim way this three hours is a Trinity experience—the Father in the hour of silence, the Son in the hour of writing, and the Holy Spirit in the hour of sharing. God speaks! We are compelled to etch it upon our hearts in writing and then we are ready to bear witness unafraid and we dare to say with Paul, "if you read my words, you will have some idea of the depths that I see in the mystery of Christ" Eph. 3, 4.

3
Scripture - Thirst

"You should give that Word your closest attention and take it as a lamp for lighting a way through the dark until the dawn comes and the morning star rises in your mind." (2 Pet 1.19)

"He is present in His Word, since it is He Himself who speaks when the Holy Scriptures are read in the Church." (Vat II Liturgy 7)

". . . when we brought the Good News to you, it came to you not only as words, but as power and as the Holy Spirit and as utter conviction . . . and it was with the joy of the Holy Spirit that you took to the gospel . . ." (1 Thess 5-6). These words of Paul's first epistle seem to ring out with even greater validity in 1971 for the contemporary people of God. "And it is still a living power among you who believe it " (1 Thess. 2, 13). Scripture is a thirst, a strangely addictive thirst—the more you drink of it the more you need. "If you but knew the gift of God and who it is that speaks to you . . . the water that I shall give will turn into a spring inside him, welling up to eternal life." (Jo. 4, 10 & 14).

It has long been repeated that prayer is a loving conversation with one whom you know loves you. Yet not a few today ask how do I know that I am not talking to myself, in an on-going dialogue between me, myself and I? Is it really an I-Thou encounter or just more I-me? There is some demythologizing and linguistic analysis that would much enrich our prayer. Language is a channel that ever needs dredging, deepening, and purifying. A metaphor that clarifies for one era, obscures for the next. There is a factuality-depth more than we dare dream in prayer as conversation. It is Scripture, the Word of God that is the reality-depth of our prayer, for "we speak to Him when we pray: we hear Him when we read the divine sayings." From the Hassidim, the Jewish mystics, there is the beautiful legend of the rabbi who would go into ecstasy every time he would utter the words "and God spoke . . ." He would become totally overwhelmed with the realization that God spoke to man!

What would happen to us if we would more deeply believe the truth—God speaks! God speaks to me! This is the heart of prayer, this is the power behind the prayer revolution of today—that God is speaking directly to me in Scripture. "If only you would listen to Him today; do not harden your hearts . . ." (Ps. 95). Vatican II did not hesitate to say, "The Church has always venerated the divine Scriptures just as she venerates the body of the Lord, since from the table of both the Word of God and of the Body of Christ she unceasingly receives and offers to the faithful the bread of life, especially in the sacred liturgy " (Revelation 21).

Revelation is revolution not through a vowel change of *o u* for *e a* but because you discover your and His "*o*h yo*u*" in it! Scripture is the divine human dialogue of the mutual *you* spoken simultaneously to each other "you!"

The technical language of the Scripture scholars is being broken open as bread to be eaten, no longer as something to be in awe with from afar.

Revelation is not a barren abstract work—it is a Father sharing all that He is with his children coming of age, growing into what He is. A word is always personal because it can exist only between persons. To be a person is to be unique, to be a secret, to be hidden, to be unknown. The more a person is, the greater the uniqueness. The greater the secret, the mystery, the hiddenness, the unknown. The greater the depth of being, the more inexhaustible the mystery. No one can know another unless the person chooses to be known, to speak a word. And to speak a word is to enter into union with another. No word is idle, every word has power, creativity. Every word is conceptive, generative, *if* the other is open to it. Every word is unitive, consecratory of the other into oneself, *if* the other listens. Existentially, actually, really, revelation does not take place unless there are two persons open to each other.

What must be the depth of the Word that the Father speaks to us in Jesus through the Spirit! His Word not only reveals Himself, it unveils us. His word is consecratory, continuing to change us more and more into His image so that we can understand more and more whatever He says to us! The Word that God speaks is deposited deeply within oneself. The womb of the mind and heart must be readied, waiting, responsive. The Word does not simply imprint itself, it imbeds itself, releases seeds that will mature in their own time. The Word always remains His Word, bears His resemblance and is creative of Him in us. It effects what it signifies and renders Him present. "He is present in His Word, since it is He Himself who speaks when the Holy Scriptures are read in the Church." (Vatican II Liturgy 7). For many it is still startling and difficult to get used to the different presences of Christ. Yet how important and far reaching it is to understand this real presence of Christ in Scripture. It is the Word of Scripture uttered by the priest that renders Christ present in Eucharist; or expressed more precisely, it is Christ who renders Himself present through the Scriptural word of the Church. Scripture is much more than a sacramental like a crucifix, ikon, statue, or holy water. Yet Scripture is not a Presence as the reserved Eucharist is. Christ is present in Scripture only when another person is present to Him. Christ is not present in the closed book, or enshrined text. The print on the page is not His presence, but whenever His word is breathed in faith, He is present, for the Word can only be His Word, it is never just a human word. Whenever the Sacred Scriptures are read and prayed in faith it is He Himself who speaks. Scripture is *the* preparation for and most real extension of the Eucharist. In a sense Scripture is a portable and mobile Eucharist. Real communion with Christ exists every time we pray Scripture. He promised us: the Spirit is His promise kept.

> "at the moment you do not know what I am doing, but later you will understand." (Jo. 13, 7). "and my word is not my own: It is the word of the one who sent me. I have said these things to you while still with you; but the advocate, the Holy Spirit, whom the Father will send in my name, will teach you everything and remind you of all I have said to you " (Jo. 14, 24—26).

Every person is a thirst for meaning, for ultimate value, for truth. Every person is a readiness to love, to follow, to give oneself to that which fills and completes the movement of its being.

> "My soul thirsts for God, the God of life; when shall I go to see the face of God... I

remember, and my soul melts within me... Deep is calling to deep... Send out your light and your truth, let these be my guide, to lead me to your holy mountain and to the place where you love." (Ps. 42). "You have seduced me, Yahweh, and I have let myself be seduced " (Jer. 20, 7).

The spirit of man intuitively reaches to its source, its ground of being. Man knows that his secret can be uncovered only through His secret. "Such knowledge is beyond my understanding, a height to which my mind cannot attain " (Ps. 139, 6). "Great are your achievements, Yahweh, immensely deep your thoughts " (Ps. 92, 5).

God finally speaks His ultimate and inexhaustible Word, "Jesus Christ, the revelation of a mystery kept secret for endless ages." (Rom. 16, 25). Paul again and again dwells upon

"the message which was a mystery hidden for generations and centuries and has now been revealed to his saints... The mystery is Christ among you, your hope of glory: this is the Christ we proclaim, this is the wisdom in which we thoroughly train everyone and instruct everyone to make them all perfect in Christ " (Col 1, 26—28).

Paul prays constantly that

"the Father of glory, give you a spirit of wisdom and *perception* of what is revealed, to bring you to *full* knowledge of him. May he enlighten the eyes of your mind so that you can see what hope His call holds for you..." (Eph. 1, 17 & 18.)

Paul wanted the Colossians to know that he

had to struggle hard for them "to stir your minds, so that your *understanding* may come to full *development*, until you really know God's secret in which all the jewels of wisdom and knowledge are hidden" (Co. 2, 2-3). Paul's prayer for his communities can hardly be contained in words,

"May He give you the power through His Spirit for your hidden self to grow strong, so that Christ may live in your hearts through faith, and then, planted in love and built on love, you will with all the saints have strength to grasp the breadth and the length, the height and the depth; until knowing the love of Christ, which is *beyond all knowledge*, you are filled with the fullness of God" (Eph. 3–16–19).

"Try to discover what the Lord wants of you" (Eph 5, 10). God is the most personal of all beings. He cannot act impersonally, anonymously, indiscriminately. Before God man is never a faceless, nameless, lonely crowd. God can only act personally, intimately, person to person. The Father can do nothing else except be Fathering.

"I have called you by your name, you are mind" (Is. 43.1) "One by one he calls His own sheep and leads them out... I know my own and my own know me, just as the Father knows me and I know the Father" (Jo. 10, 3 & 14). "I call you friends, because I have made known to you everything I have learnt from my Father" (Jo. 15, 15). "I have made your name known to them and will continue to make it known" (Jo. 17, 26).

Paul almost leaps off the page with his exuberance when he attempts to describe to the Corinthians "the hidden wisdom of God."

> "We teach what Scripture calls 'the things that no eye has seen and no ear has heard, things beyond the mind of man, all that God has prepared for those who love him'" (I Cor. 2, 9).

To enter into Scripture is a Zacchaeus experience. Something in us is "anxious to see what kind of man Jesus is." Finding the time and going apart or calling two or three together is like "running ahead and climbing a sycamore tree to catch a glimpse of Jesus who was to pass that way." But what a moment it is when Jesus looks up and calls out our name, "Come down. Hurry, because I must be your guest this day" (Lu 19, 1-10). Scripture is autobiographical! He who called us out of nothingness, who is with us on the way, who is the omega of our journey, alone knows our inmost self and alone can speak to our heart. He speaks our name as no one else can. He speaks our person, for each of us is a word that He has begun to utter and will never be finished until we are one with Him. He speaks to us uniquely as no one else dares to speak.

The Word is fruitful, "the word that goes from my mouth does not return to me empty, without carrying out my will and succeeding in what it was sent to do" (Is. 55, 11). His Word is a dawning light ever expanding and filtering into the daily life experiences, opening us to His presence in them. The news of the day enters into the eternal news.

The Word of hope and promise is now flesh forever in Eucharist, in the Church, in the hearts of men. In the Word men keep the Word and become the Word proclaimed. Through the Word, each man becomes Gospel.

In the words of Vatican II, "There is a growth in the understanding of the realities and the words which have been handed down. This happens through the contemplation and study made by believers who treasure these things in their heart, through the intimate, understanding of spiritual things they experience " (Revelation No. 8).

"Just as the life of the Church grows through persistent participation in the Eucharistic mystery, so we may hope for a new surge of spiritual vitality from intensified veneration for God's word, which lasts forever " (Revelation 26).

4
Penance:
Return Of The Heart

"I carry your heart. I carry it in my heart."

— e. e. cummings

To celebrate liturgy is an authentic way to experience that Christ carries the heart of each of us in his own heart. And to receive Christ means that we receive not only His heart but the hearts of all others. Surely in this lies a way of understanding the meaning of the sacrament of penance, which might be best expressed as a return of the heart.

The theological literature on penance has been enriched by writers of the stature of Karl Rahner, Bernard Haring, and Charles Curran, and we have, as a result, an enlarged understanding of its significance for our own day. I do not propose to speak so much of theology as of experiences and to invite you to reflect with me and to think into the mystery of penance. Each one of us is an authority on penance. We have long lived it and we cannot have lived so long and celebrated the mystery so frequently without in some way becoming experts, authorities, persons with much experience. Living itself is an experience of penance. One thing is certain; penance is alive, and anything alive changes. One of our deepest hopes is that we can change, because penance is concerned with change —not the kind of change which we sometimes call spontaneous, which we can so easily speak of in words, but a change at a much deeper level of being and action.

The sacrament of penance, or penance itself which we are experiencing today has an aura of Spring about it. There are certain seasons, certain times, certain patterns to the Christian life even as there were in

Christ's life; and we follow those patterns. Christ was buried. He arose. And the truths of Christ will not be unlike himself. There are forgotten truths in our faith, in our life experiences, which have been laid aside and buried. We can become so familiar with particular realities that we forget the language. Even our relationship with Christ can be diminished. But there is always a resurrection, always a rising. They are like bulbs which lie buried and forgotten in winter's chill grip, but still are *there*, waiting, until, mysteriously, Spring comes and we discover them. There is an expectancy about Spring. There is an expectancy about penance. It is a new discovery for each of us, something which we have not wholly experienced before and it is important that we understand the why of this. Penance is ancient, yet ever new. There is a "today" even though we have had a "yesterday." There is in us always a newness and an aliveness.

When we were young, when we were very small, we saw things in a particular way. Then we grew, grew up, developed in many areas. There is, however, a certain stabilization that takes place, and if our growth did not in some way level out, we would be sixty, eighty, perhaps one hundred feet tall. Imagine the problems of the environment then! In our early years we thought that when our physical growth had levelled off and stabilized that our growth was finished. Yet it had only begun.

When we grew to a certain size perhaps we returned to the school where we once attended kindergarten and the first primary grades. The old neighborhood looked almost quaint. It looked so small because we had grown so large. This physical growth is a true growth; yet it is after we have achieved it that the real growth takes place, the growth of mind and heart and soul, by which we are led into and beyond the senses, into the arts, literature, history, philosophy and faith. Even in our day of specialization, as one follows ever more deeply his specialization it becomes in some strange, little understood way, narrower and narrower until at a mysterious moment it opens into a wholly new horizon. At such a moment one is made aware that this universe is too vast for the mind to grasp.

It is then, in this experience that man slowly and painfully becomes little. It is then that he begins to acquire real knowledge, real humility; that he moves toward maturity. I think that we are on the edge of this kind of growth. No longer do we need the pride and arrogance of adolescence. This humility, or perhaps humiliation has touched all of us. We become aware of an unsureness, the unsureness of maturity; we begin at last to know that we do not know and perhaps will never know all that we so much desire to know. A profound transformation, a growth, an evolution now takes place in us. Now we begin to discover truths which we really had never known, yet were there awaiting our discovery, our awakening to their being. We never knew them at all, we never saw them; they were there but we did not see them. We have heard about these ideas, concepts, truths, perhaps even talked about them. Now, however, in this new experience we have no word, no thought, no concept, perhaps not even a theology.

Now we become much more people of experienced awareness and all must be initialed with our initial and be ours in our unique way; otherwise, we belong to no one, nor do the truths belong to us. We begin to know ourselves in a new context of spiritual knowledge. I think this experience is true especially of the mysteries of Christ, the mystery of church—which is essentially mystery—the mystery of penance, the mystery of celibacy; and the mystery of human action, the mystery of your act and of my act. When we do something, it is irreversible. We never can step back and undo it.

There is an act which we call a promise and that act nails down the future. It is an absurdity because who can speak for his future; and yet a promise *is* possible and is perhaps the most significant act a person makes; for we know even as we make the act that it is unpredictable; and even beyond that, any act has an anonymity in its effect. We do not know what effect it will have, how long it will endure, what changes it will create.

Humanly speaking, the past, the future, even the present is so much not in our grasp. Yet in all of our acts the mystery of Christ speaks to each one of these realities. He speaks to the events of the past, reversing what we have done in the act of forgiveness and of penance, in the act of promise in the future which is involved in the penance, the metanoia, the change that we are seeking.

The Gospel very simply summarizes Christ's beginning, "The time is fulfilled, the kingdom is at hand. Repent, believe in the gospel." How ancient those words are and how new; yet who has heard them? Who has heard them and put them to life? *This* says something about the mystery of Christ to us and the mystery of His church which can never be separated from Him. To think of the church without Christ is to miss the mystery of both. So we move in this deep awareness into the inwardness of Christian mystery; into a knowing; into, finally, a meaning of penance.

And penance, what is it? It is a hunger, a hunger for change, it is a hunger for newness, a hunger for life, for growth, it is a hunger for wholeness and holiness, it is a hunger for experience. Most of all, I think, it is a hunger for being with and to and for. It is a relationship that is being sought. It is a togetherness. It is profoundly significant that the command of Christ was, "Repent." Why did He not begin with Eucharist? Is the Eucharist not enough? Was it enough for Christ? He began with, "Repent"; He concluded with Eucharist. It is interesting to recall the briefly recorded conversations of Christ with His disciples. One day Our Lord asked them, "Who do you say I am?" It is always interesting, both the questions of Christ, and the commands of Christ, because they are so personal, because they are asked directly of us throughout the whole of our life, and because these are the call He gives to us. He asked, "Who do you say I am?" To answer for the whole group, one volunteered—Peter, and he called back who he was. At the end of Our Lord's mission, after the resurrection, He spoke to Peter again but this time He spoke his name, "Simon Peter, do you love Me?"—not once, not twice, but three times. By name, He called him out by name! "Simon Peter, do you love me?" and as a consequence of Peter's answer, He gave another command. He said, "Feed, feed My sheep—" strengthen your brethren.

Long ago you all made a commitment or profession and how many times have you made confession since. What is the relationship between profession—confession? You cannot find it in the dictionary, but I think there is a very necessary correlation between profession and confession. Peter's profession of faith and Peter's confession of love—this is what penance is all about. Really, sin is a secondary thing. Sin is unimportant to Christ.

Penance is about a change, a change in our capacity to love. You made your final profession in words and we are all moving toward our final confession. Each one of us has his own history of penance. Just imagine trying to go over your confessions the last year or five years or ten years; imagine forty years of confessions, and how many confessions have yet to be made?

Confession: we know the confessions of Jeremiah in the Old Testament, about the *mirabilia Dei,* the wonderful things of God; the confessions of St. Augustine have disappointed many a reader who was looking for true confessions and there is so little there—eating a few pears, an illegitimate child. Really all he is talking about is the first extraordinary discovery and the ongoing discovery of the love of God for him and the power it effected in him. This is why we can speak of his confessions. Penance is first of all a confession, a song of praise to God. How unfortunate we are. We so often have said and perhaps still do say, "I cannot find anything to confess." Well, even if we did, it would be merely a partial confession because the first thing about penance is to find something, to find the love that one has received, to sing about it, to confess it. Penance is first of all an act of prayer and of worship, of thanksgiving, a recognition, a discovering of the wonderful love of God for us. But that is only part of it because it is only in the strength of this love that there can be sin. If one has not yet tasted or seen or felt something of the love of God, then he cannot sin because sin is correlative to love, and there cannot be any sin except in the context of love because sin does not exist except in the non-response to love. Penance is a discovery of what love is and what it is to love.

A friend once commented, "In our community there are so many, almost everyone, who are ready to forgive. There is so much forgiveness but there is no one who can confess her need for forgiveness." It is so easy to forgive. Did anyone ever confront you with the words, "I forgive you?" Have you ever been forgiven by another person, a second or third or fourth or twentieth time? The words, "I forgive," do not make any difference. You can come to me and tell me you are sorry and I can say I am sorry, too—about the book you lost or about the car that got dented, but that does not change. You can tell me you are sorry about the way you got angry and what you called me, and I can say, "I forgive you," but what happens when we say that word? Can we forgive? When we say, "I forgive," we are not talking about the action of God, we are not talking about the grace of Christ or the word of the church, we are saying, "I am trying not to respond to you as you deserve." That is what we ordinarily mean, and implicitly, there is a warning, "Do not let it happen again," because when it does happen again, we remind them, "How many times?" For-giveness? There are not many of us who are capable of forgiveness. There is no one of us who is capable of forgiveness in the sense that God forgives and Christ forgives, because when Christ forgives, He is not saying He is not going to respond to us as we deserve but He reaches into us, to the very roots of that which makes us the irascible persons we are. He does something if we let Him, if we are ready to be healed, to be touched and to be cured. No person can forgive sin. We can empathize with people, we can say we are sorry that they are the miserable creatures they are, but we cannot change them unless we have the capacity to love them with the love of Christ. Otherwise they are untouched by our forgiveness and this is why there is a need and a hunger to be freed from our incapacity to love and not simply to be excused and accepted and remain un-changed.

In the great mystery of Christ's death and resurrection it is the sacrament of penance that enables us in some way to get in touch with Him because without getting in touch with Him we cannot do His work. There is a strange misunderstanding in those who feel that the Eucharist is enough, that they can ignore Our Lord's call to repent and forget Our Lord's suffer-ing and death. It is as if in some way I can forgive myself, can just tell Him I am sorry or we can tell one another, "I forgive you, forget about it." In our non-response to love, our inability to love we experience the fact that we cannot heal, that we do not cure. As someone said, it is not so much that the community or church has hurt them, but it has not healed them and that is why they can no longer suffer in this way. It is a partial truth perhaps, but it is a truth. So often we cannot put this need for healing into words but we do expect, we do expect something. Some of our older brethren in Christ are not, I think, too far off in their intuition about the relationship between penance and Eucharist, penance and community; and I think I would say that there is a deep connection in diminishment of community with infrequency of and diminishment of penance.

The sacrament, the life of penance which is but the life of Christ lived out continually is the most personal of all the sacraments, the most intense and, therefore, the most difficult. Perhaps it is the last sacrament we are ready for because it demands so much of us; it demands such maturity, it demands such a capacity to suffer, the most terrible kind of suffering, to really learn who we are. We will do anything to escape that kind of suffering, that kind of anguish. Who of us is really ready to face the living God? There is so much we do in our life to prevent this happening. We talk of good faith, we even have many theologies, but who of us really wants to know himself as the Lord knows him? We do not have many temptations. It is the saints who are the primary witnesses to faith, not the theologians who are the primary witnesses—the saints, unlettered, undoctoral but primary witnesses to love.

We do not get tempted too often to express our sorrow in the dramatic gesture of a Mary Magdalen. We do not too often weep over our sins, prostrate ourselves before the Eucharist or the Christian community and confess what we are. We have forgotten and perhaps at times we do not even have the capacity any longer because it has been so underexercised. Yet the life of Christ and the reality of man speak out, and we find an extraordinary emergence today from beyond those who are called to their public witness to the mystery of Christ. We find the phenomena of penance and confession and public confession in those "outside." We see it in Alcoholics Anonymous, we see it in Synanon groups, in sensitivity groups, encounter groups, where the first thing persons do is to repent, to bare their souls on the guts level and expose who they are. It is an extraordinary thing to experience our poverty, our honesty and in so many ways our nothingness and it gives a kind of freedom which no kind of game can ever give us. It is something like those who are or who have been in a mental hospital where there are no games left any more and all they can be is real.

The Lord does not accuse us, the Lord

does not call to mind our sins: we are the only ones who remember them. The Lord simply asks us again and again, "Do you love Me?"

Today one is often questioned on the frequency of confession. I think it is important to see the sacrament of penance in terms of the totality of the Christian life; it is not something that can have its significance only in isolation and only in terms of sin. There was a valid aspect, I think, to the intuition and practice of the church in encouraging and calling her people to confession regularly and I am sure it was not so much in terms of their need for absolution from sin but more in terms of confession of the praise of God, and for a deeper understanding of their responsibility to bear the sins of others.

There was an extraordinary article in *Time* magazine in February on environment and I would certainly commend it for your spiritual reading. In this article some undoubtedly pessimistic experts say that we have so interfered with the ecological system of the world that it is irreversible and human life cannot continue on this planet beyond 200 years. This was just a small portion of the article but it drove home the reality that the smallest atom has a history, has an effect that goes so far beyond itself that it is almost incalculable what any act of ours can do. I think it speaks so strongly about the mystery of human community and how we affect one another not only for a moment but have an ongoing effect; and that nothing is really lost. It speaks so strongly to the awareness we must carry within ourselves of the responsibility Christ took upon Himself for the whole world and for the sin and inability and absence of love in so many. It speaks to the fact that to follow Christ's likeness we, too, must be totally concerned with the conversion and transformation of people and where there is not love, to put love.

When we go to confession, we go first of all to recognize that we are sinners and no one of us gets beyond that basic fact—that we are sinners even though saved. The remarkable thing in the testimony and history of the saints is that the more one grows in his experience of the love of Christ, the more he realizes how much this love is absent in himself. He is drawn to the sacrament of penance out of his life experience; not from some external "you ought to" or "you should," but because it becomes more and more a need. There is a hunger for it which cannot be satisfied by anything less than being plunged into this mystery of Christ.

St. Catherine of Siena spoke deeply of this mystery in words that sound strange and rather strong to us—"Being washed in the blood of Christ." At the same time, these are words that are deeply Scriptural —Isaian—the Suffering Servant—the mystery of the blood of Christ. We need to be deeply penetrated with them. We need to be aware that when we go to confession, which is a profession of faith, a confession of love, and a deep experience of a need to be touched by Christ and to be transformed by Him, something takes place even though there is no way of validating it in terms of a pragmatic principle. We cannot measure it on the day to day level just as life cannot be measured on that particular level. There are movements within ourselves that perhaps take a long time before they can make their manifestation in our nervous system, on the tip of our fingers. When we go to confession we need to be aware that a whole community is involved, not just a particular house but everyone who is in our lives.

One of the problems of frequent confession is the confessor. I think we are all caught in this together. Our theology is usually behind our experience, and there are many priests who have had great difficulty in finding confessors themselves. I do not think there is more than one in thirty priests who has a confessor, has a spiritual director. There has been a great impoverishment because we have not recognized nor developed this charism. I do think there is a special apostolate that the Christian can exercise in this regard. I would almost say there is a reality to "bringing up Father." I do not mean that facetiously. One of the primary sources of a priest's grace and growth is his ministry and I do not think this is affected more deeply than in the sacrament of penance, where we have a Christian who comes to con-celebrate the sacrament; he is not there passively to accept something, but is there truly exercising his baptismal priesthood, making the sacrament present. The Eucharist exists without our presence, but the sacrament of penance never happens without us. How often have we prayed for our confessor? How often have we done penance for him? In the Middle Ages, the priest and penitent would go before the altar and kneel together in prayer for a long time. The priest had to fast before celebrating the sacrament. I think we sometimes have lost the sense of the mystery and the tremendous gift of God forgiving us our sins in the grace of Christ, in the word of the church.

How frequently we should approach the sacrament of penance is difficult to say, but like most things we learn by practice. How do we learn spontaneity in prayer? The idea that spontaneity is saying the first thing that comes to your mind is an illusion, a fantasy. It is not prayer. Spontaneous prayer, spontaneous penance comes from long hard effort. We learn a habit by an action done over and over again until it becomes almost co-natural, almost a very part of our being and we pray not out of the top of our mind, but out of the bottom of our heart. We do not know that yet, we have not learned it. The world is calling upon us in a way it has never called upon us before. It is calling upon us to be persons, and even more, to be Christians—to be of Christ and to give of Christ. How long does it take to discover penance? How long does it take to make a good confession? How long does it take to make a good communion? When was the last time we really received and responded to the Eucharist? How many times do we make a good communion in a year?

I do not think we can celebrate the sacrament of penance too often. Each day the church needs to be able to enter into Holy Thursday and into the death and resurrection of Christ. Each day the world has need of redemption. One of the Fathers of the church once said penance is the "baptism of our own tears." Baptism, we might say, is being plunged into Christ which becomes forever indelible once we are baptized, but penance is the matter of saying, "I." It is hard for us to say "I," "I am." This is what penance calls us to—to take the responsibility of being "me" and being Christian and being Christ—of being able to speak as Paul would speak, "Be imitators of me."

5
Be Eucharists

What we love can be looked at so long that it becomes invisible. Suddenly we look at it and it has become strange and we no longer know what it is.

The person I love can be seen so often that he becomes invisible. Suddenly I look at him and he has become a stranger and I no longer know who he is. "C'est La vie!" That is life, and it is a sadness. It might be my own father, my brother, my close friend. I have changed and am no longer the same person; what was, no longer is. Fathers, brothers, friends have to be discovered again and again. All human relation and connection grows and diminishes, rises, and falls. Life must be breathed together or it ceases.

What is true of human love is true of inner life of the spirit. Today perhaps this is most true about the Eucharist. For many the Eucharist has become an embarrassment. We do not know how to respond to it. We feel awkward before Him, sometimes guilty for lack of response. There is much ambivalence in these transitional days—we are outgrowing one relationship aspect and have not yet grown into another.

The old language of the Eucharist— "presence," "person," "love," "growth," "mystery," "dialogue" has been absorbed by the field of human interaction and interpersonal relationships. And this is a valid development from a possibility to a human actuality. Our Lord told us what would come to be, but without the experience it was only words, words which could not be understood until it came to pass. Much of the language of the Eucharist has been actualized in human experience and now out of our deepened human interpersonal relations we find a new depth of meaning in the Eucharist. Eucharist is no longer static and abstract but dynamic and experiential.

Personal presence is deeply significant to us today for ourselves as much as for others. What we do is so much less than what we are. The person, his inner and outer being, not the job, role, background is the significant. Only a small fraction of our whole person-totality can ever be expressed in any work, role, relationship. "I can't really put myself into it" is an old expression, but it continues to have many new implications. "I'm not really with it." We can be present in many different ways. We can be present in a room or to a room; we can be present to a person or with him. There can be physical presence and personal absence. We can be so present to ourselves that we are not present to another.

The Eucharist is personal presence. There is an incarnateness and presence limited in time and space. The Eucharist is a here-and-nowness, not a everywhere-ness all at once. The Incarnation took on limitations of time and place—Jesus was only one place at a time. The Eucharist is under a similar limitation—He is not everywhere all at once in the same way. He is not equally present to everyone, everywhere—any more than we are. Wherever He is present, He is present as person, as relating, as interacting.

He effects our presence; we affect His presence. In Eucharist He is present not because we think of Him, or because of attentiveness, consciousness, or awareness. He is present not even because of an act of faith on our part. He is present because He intends to be present through the sacramental act of the priest, a visible presence that continues when the priest and community are no longer present. Christ is present in our churches not as the altar is present but as personal presence. The stone or wooden altar never effects our presence. Jesus in Eucharist always effects our presence. We never effect the altar in our churches, but we do effect Christ's presence. Christ is present to us each in a unique way, according to our faith and love and according to His love and mercy which is unique for each of us. He is present personally as person to Himself, to the Spirit and to the Father. He is present personally to each of us as persons, as knowing us by name, calling us into being and drawing us on to Himself in glory.

He can never be simply present statically. He is always there as being for us, moving to us, reaching out toward us. There is within each of us a hunger for His personal presence. His presence in others is not enough—no more than an acquaintance of my best friend would be a substitute for my best friend. Presence of others can fill me to a degree, but there still remains a hunger for Him that remains unfulfilled by them alone.

This new consciousness of the Eucharist can have tidal effects on our whole spirituality. It is not something taught but something learned out of our new and deeper experience of ourselves and others. Our new appreciation of the human word has opened Scripture to us in ever-deepening ways. The Incarnation is God's excess. Yet even more incredible is His personal union with each of us. The Eucharist is the bridge between these two mysteries of God's excess of love. Eucharist is the guarantee of Incarnation and Indwelling union. Eucharist is an excess and an extravagance of love beyond the human imagination, yet it is a kenosis, an emptying out. Sacraments are finite, limited in space and time. There is a presence of Christ beyond Eucharist, beyond Word, people, minister, and even Church. He is not limited but we are. There must be deep reverence, deep love before these mysteries or we easily become arrogant and think we know God and diminish Him to our own limitations.

What Jesus can teach us of presence through Eucharist! What we wouldn't do to be able to take in a personal appearance of Jesus! How easy for us to become a Zaccheus—"anxious to see what kind of man Jesus was," "to run ahead and climb a sycamore tree to catch a glimpse of Jesus." Consider then the way Jesus was present to him! Of all of the people along the way, it was before him that Jesus stopped, looked up and called by name, "Zaccheus, come down. Hurry, because I must stay at your house today." We can never stop wondering at the depth of Jesus' presence to people in His days on earth. He drew so many to Him and by the identical presence repulsed so many. The poor and humble, the seekers of truth and goodness knew the current that carried them to Him. The proud and arrogant feared that same current and it set off the need to destroy that presence that indicted them.

Yet the presence of Jesus in our midst is even greater today; otherwise He would not have left us. "It is better for you that I go." The presence of Christ with us today is the presence of Christ in His risen Glory, the pleroma, the fullness that fills the whole earth, the presence that Paul experienced in a dramatic way on the road to Damascus. It is Jesus who has indissolubly united Himself with each of us through baptism, penance, and Eucharist.

The new consciousness of the Eucharist is the source, center, and focus of the rediscovery of prayer. Prayer has left the periphery of contemporary man and has moved to the core of his life. The prayer of modern man has deepened so much that one needs a new language to describe it. And this prayer has gravitated to the Eucharist as its center and source. Prayer is the deepest way of being present to oneself. The more we are present to Him, the more we become present to ourselves and the more we *are* present to ourselves, the more we can be present to others. To be present to Jesus is to step deeper into ourselves, not step out of ourselves.

What must happen to our prayer when Jesus comes to pray with us and in us! A whole new power to pray comes to us in Eucharist. We cry out, "Lord, I am not worthy that you should come to me—Your word is enough!" Yet words are not enough for Him. He comes to make Himself at home in us and the Father comes with Him! No wonder that the desert fathers described Christian prayer as listening deeply within ourselves to the prayer Jesus utters to His Father.

No man by himself can know his own spirit. You need someone to be with you as you go down into your depths. Only Jesus can reveal the image in which you were made. Only Jesus can be the light and open you to the life He calls you to. Only Jesus can free you from your inability to love and can show you the way.

Each day we hear His command, "Do this in remembrance of me." This is the most startling word of the Eucharist—that each Christian is to learn to consecrate, to be drawn into Christ's action so deeply that he becomes a Eucharist! We are to parallel Christ; what He did with His life we are to do with our lives. What a mystery this is, to consecrate ourselves, to become Eucharists! This is what the Christian life is all about; this is the ultimate conclusion and action of following Christ—to be body given, to be blood shed. To consecrate is to sacrifice, to die, to pass over into a new world, a new life, a new level and depth of existence and consciousness. It is easy to offer Christ's sacrifice, to be an innocent bystander and to say, "This is *his* body, this is *his* blood." But when we begin to pray deeply the two-edged real words of consecration, "This is *my* body, this is *my* blood," something begins to happen. Those awesome words of His are stamped deeper and deeper into consciousness. One either honestly stops praying those words or slowly begins to become what the words are. Those words of consecration are not mere words on anyone's lips. They are a great action, an immense giving over, an unconditional abandonment. They are a promise and vow committing one's life and presence to another totally until death. It is not easy to make ourselves present to another for a whole life. It demands a high concentration of oneself and all the enduring consequences. Only Eucharist enables us to change ourselves into another, giving ourselves into His hands. The Eucharist is a continuum, an ongoing action, of what He and I are doing and becoming. Eucharist is not only His presence with me but my presence with Him. Wherever He is, there I am; wherever He goes, I go with Him. Eucharist is the sign, the visible witness of what we have done, what we are doing and what we will become. In Eucharist we consecrate each day, each person, each event, hallowing it, firing it, filling it with His Spirit, His presence, being taken up with Him.

Again and again Jesus asked His disciples, "Do you understand what I have done?" We answer the question like the disciples, "Yes!" Yet we, like them, understand so little. Our threshold for love is low—if love is too great, we somehow numb ourselves and our consciousness to it lest it overwhelms us. We are capable of only so much love, so much pain. Eucharist can never be more intelligible than Bethlehem and Calvary. The Eucharist will always be beyond the furthest reaches of man's imagination: a scandal and stumbling block for many, the greatest reality of love for those of faith.

The Eucharist is daily Incarnation, incarnation in us, the most concrete and specific evidence given to man that God is Emmanuel, that He dwells among men. The beginning of the Incarnation was unilateral; the Father took the initiative, He took the first giant step. Eucharist, the on-going incarnation is bilateral; it is an interaction between God and man. The initiative now rests with man to bring Christ among men. It is the people of God's great daily act of faith, of hope, and of love. Time does not decrease the mystery of God dwelling among men. It is as much mystery, surprise, and embarrassment today as was the prefigurement of the Ark of the Covenant to the Jews.

The wonders of God so easily overreach the threshold of our consciousness that we seem to be inert stone and rock. So much happens so quickly; it is over before we begin to get into it.

The Eucharist is life, our daily life that comes to us each day freshly made. Like our life, it is a continuum, yet like our life it is new and unique each day. We will, as we live our today, live it as we live Eucharist!

Eucharist is the 2,000 year-old evidence of His faith in us, our faith in Him. "I am with you all days." These words of Christ are not metaphors, subjective potentialities; His words are incarnate among men in the objective reality of the Eucharist. It is the gift of the Father, the power of the Spirit compelling us to remember and to understand. Yet the invitations to the banquet go unheeded; we fail to recognize who it is that speaks to us. He still charges His disciples to eat, to reveal their unknown hunger to Him; He changes them to get them to eat, to reveal their unknown hunger to them.

The Eucharist is not a symbol alone; it is more than a conceptual word, it is a "dabar," an event, a collision of God with man. He comes, He really comes to us. In that moment we come into Incarnation, death, and resurrection. All of Him becomes ours, we become His. All our sacraments become operational. All of my life, my world, my people become actuated.

I offer this bread and wine of the earth, this moment of human history, the people of my day and He mysteriously gives them back to me not as me but as Him! I am never more immersed in time and space as in Eucharist! In fact, I am so immersed that I break into the third dimension deeper than time or space, into the dimension of God Himself. Every Eucharist contains and enfolds all the Eucharists I have ever celebrated and anticipates all that are yet to be celebrated. There is a presence of His whole body in and beyond time and space.

He feeds me with His own hunger. He stretches me toward the limits of His own consciousness. I pass through the walls of the senses and the dimness of the mind across the world and grow more and more in the lives of all His people. And they grow into me and enter deeper and deeper into my consciousness, becoming "one body, one Spirit, one hope, one Lord, one baptism, one faith, one God and Father of all."

I live now, not I but they live in me. His members, His people live in me and I live in them. The Father and all that He is and that is of Him comes into me and I enter into Him. We are drawn into the Divine Center that holds all of us in existence. His descent is an ascension into that disappearing point that opens out into the pleroma of all that is.

"These were only pale reflections of what was coming: the reality is Christ.

Col. 2:18

"And now the life you have is hidden with Christ in God . . . and He is your life."

Col. 3:3

"There is only Christ:
    He is Everything
    and He is in everything."

Col. 3:11

6

Reverence

The whole of our Christian life is spent in discovering that we are Jesus. We can never learn this deeply enough. We spend our lives celebrating Eucharist, celebrating Mass. In some way, this is all we have to do—to remember, to realize, to anticipate who He is in order to know who we are. To ask the question, who He is, is to ask the question, who we are.

Each one of us is an orchestra all our own, an orchestra in which there are brass, reed and wind, stringed and percussion instruments. We are constantly being played upon by the many people who come and breathe a moment in our lives, pluck a chord here or there, strike us in some new way. There is a symphony; there are notes that are being drawn from us each day. There are movements in our life that most of the time we are unaware of; there is an ongoing development and we need time to reflect upon it. We are constantly drawing one another, enriching one another. Every word that has ever been uttered by anyone is carried somehow within everyone. We are carried by everyone who has ever heard our desire, our hope, our longing. It is amazing how much of each other we carry within ourselves— the word of love, the word of anger, the tears, the exuberance, the anguish, the ecstasy, the deep prints that we have made —the voice prints, the fingerprints, at times, perhaps—the footprints, the nailprints in one another. We grow in the most unusual ways in people, ways which we would least expect. How we grow, where we would like to grow and when we actually find ourselves growing are part of the mystery of community. Sometimes our most idle word has been the most meaningful word in another person. We are a mosaic of each other. The community reality and possibilities are far from being actualized. The greatest reverence is between two people and this has not been traveled by many people. It must be reciprocal.

"Every sin of man will be forgiven except against the Holy Spirit," except that against love. That is the only sin. What is it to love?—simply to recognize and to affirm. What is it all about, this matter of living and loving?—perhaps it is expressed very simply in the words themselves, the word "live" and the word "love." It is a matter of the two vowels: the "i" and the "o". To live is to open the "i", our human eye and the *I* of the person to the "Oh!" of the other, and we never finish doing that. Community is never established totally and completely because no one is ever finished. We are not finished as persons, and the community, which is really a matter of learning how to live and love together, is never finished. We can never say, "Now we have community." As Jesus is infinitely capable of being discovered in us, the community is always capable of more growth as we are capable of more growth. We are called to realize that each one of us is truly an existence of Jesus—to discover Him in one another, to enable Him to come to be. Community is always His mystery.

Community demands reverence. Community means to discover reverence toward one another, to discover a deeper reverence toward ourself. We need to discover more fully that mystery of what we are, because our sense of reverence and mystery toward ourselves will be the measure of our sense of reverence and mystery toward one another. What is it to experience reverence?—to be carried away by God, to be carried away by nature, to be carried away by another person? Reverence has something to do with holiness and wholeness. Reverence is a word that ordinarily is ascribed to God alone. We have reverence for Him and to speak about reverence in regard to ourselves is to speak of the relation He has with us and we with Him. It is a mysterious relationship—it is the mystery of God giving. He gives so much; He gives so much of Himself when He loves. He doesn't love as we do, who can love with such a small part of ourselves. God cannot but love totally and completely. There is nothing that can resist His love, except ourselves. We ask for a piece of sand and He gives us a beach. We ask for a drop of water and He gives us the ocean. We ask for time and He gives us life eternal. And it is so easy for us to fall in love with the gift and forget the giver. This is why there is always a danger, a subtle danger, of idolatry—to adore that which is not God, but only the echo; to fall in love with the painting and not to know the painter; to fall in love with the music and not know the heart out of which this music has come; and we, ourselves, to fall in love with our own life and yet not know from whom it has come, where it is going or how it is sustained. Yet, it is always important to discover love for oneself, for without this, there is no capacity to fall in love with Him.

An experience of reverence, is an experience of tension. Reverence is in tension with idolatry. Sometimes God seems almost to tempt us to idolatry. We make so many mistakes because we do not look at creation deeply enough and people deeply enough. In some way, the radiant glory of another person, as all of nature, is the glory of earth, and each one of us is the glory of God; we are called to discern this radiant glory of God in one another. We have all seen paintings of the saints. Raphael liked to paint great tableaux of all the saints together. It is one thing to paint these saints after they have died, but another to collect them while they are still alive. We need to reflect on our holiness and wholeness, not because of our absence of sin, but in spite of our sin, just because God loves that way. We have to believe that He loves us so much that we are holy, and holy in a way that we give holiness to others—that we have been loved so much that it overflows into a gift to others. The love which nourishes us enables us to nourish others; and this love continues like running water to flow into our lives, and from our lives, into the lives of others.

Reverence is the natural virtue of the child. A child is always filled with reverence but this is an innocence not a virtue. A child cannot help being filled with awe and reverence because everything is so totally new, everything is fresh. In reality that is our experience again and again—everything is new. We so often fail to look at one another. Each day we have a new face, one we have never seen before.

The virtue of reverence is really the virtue of humility, of humus, of the earth. We need to get close to the earth and to see the grass come out of the ground. The awareness of new life helps us to discover the newness in us. The newness outside of us helps us discover the universe within us—the infinite capacity we have for God.

We need everything that *is* to actualize our capacity for God. As an exercise, it is good at times to write down what has come to be in us, what has been born in us, what is new and fresh and alive that was not there, say a year ago,—what has come into our consciousness. Much is already present in us of which we are not yet conscious and it may be a year or five years before we will perceive them or someone else will tell us of them. It is the mystery of discovery— discovering as a little child, first, things; then the wonder of things; then the wonder of words for things and words for people; and then the symbols that express that which cannot be expressed. This is one of the most important experiences of reverence. The opposite of reverence is not simply jealousy but violence. There is no in-between. There are a lot of subtle forms of violence today, but the saddest kind of violence is the violence done to ourselves. This violence is in each of us; we call it sin. Sometimes it is not culpable; it is just a violence to ourselves because we do not appreciate, we do not reverence who we are.

How often we can be entranced by a scene in nature, can be awed and humbled by it, or by a painting or a piece of music, but can be insensitive to one another. We can be awed by a mountain or a vista but not by what we see in one another. All these things shall pass. The hills are still living as the crust of the earth is living. The mountains at one time were plains, perhaps valleys, they will change; only we continue to live on. Each of us, in some way, creates landscapes for one another. We create valleys or places of rest. We create vistas, far horizons, mountains, valleys and plains. We are water or desert. Deep beyond the hills, beyond the deserts, beyond the valleys is the mystery of that altar which He has erected in each one of us, where He has met us, where we meet Him and where in the depth of our being we meet each other. Reverence is not something uniform, the same for everyone. We come to reverence one another's sense of reverence which will differ with each.

Reverence is very close to her sister hope, a vital aspect of community as well. Hope does not force. Hope knows that time is essential, waiting is necessary, patience is to be learned. Hope can believe in time because it knows that everything that is, is an excess. Everything that is, is more than could have been expected, more than is deserved. How good of God and how mysterious, how wonderful and how strange for God to make a dog, to make flowers (they seem so unnecessary), to make blue skies and green grass. The excess of life! There is no person that can demand anything to be. Everything is above and beyond that which would have been expected. This is the experience of hope: from the experience and the reverence that *I am,* ' and being overwhelmed with this mystery by the continuing mystery of the birth of what *we are*, there is a hope that what is, will mysteriously continue to be. One does not have to worry, one does not have to be afraid, one can live in hope because the very act of living is an exercise of hope.

Exupery once spoke of fraternity and equality as distinct. "The conditions of the fraternity you seek derive not from equality, for equality is consummated of God alone. Brotherhood is a recompense. It stems from your acceptance of a hierarchy and from the temple that you build for each." Fraternity or community does not mean everyone must be alike or respond in the same way. Some can sing, others cannot, some can cook and others cannot, some can write poetry and others cannot.

Fraternity demands a reverence of discovering the uniqueness of Jesus' act of creation in another person. That demand means we have to learn what we do not know. It means we have to learn a personality that is not ours. There is nothing more difficult than to learn a new personality, yet nothing more closely Christian because to be Christian means that we have always to be expanding our personality range. It is difficult to experience another person. We think we do, but it is easy merely to experience ourselves in other people. This is what we do most of the time. Why do I like you?—because you have the intelligence to like me. We are very compatible. Even the heathen do that. But our love, our fraternity must be more than that. Christians are those who are marked by their diversity, who are marked by the lame and the crippled and the blind and the dumb and the stupid and the poor. We are a mighty, motley group as St. Paul would say. What do you have? What can you boast about? Not much, except *He* who is our Savior and *He* who is with us.

We are extremely prejudiced. We do not have a word for it. It is like racism on an individual level. There is no one quite like me. "Speak my language or I'll never understand you." It is hard for us to break out of that narrowness, but that is what we are intended to do. We must find a point of connection with each, an identifying point, recognize something of ourselves in that other person, enabling us to say, "I know your pain; I know your joy." When we read Scripture and look at the diversity of the people in Our Lord's life, every conceivable kind of person was there. We see His evident ability to be in contact with people so that everyone found it easy to be with Him. He facilitated people. One may be too strong for another person. Most of us are fairly knowledgeable in helping people or doing things for people. Too often what we fail to do is allow others to reach us, to teach us, to be gift to us, to experience our need for them. We learn this truth with great pain because we spend much of our lives trying to become independent. When we reach this point, we find out how inadequate autonomy is. Then we have to start all over again, allowing people to know how incomplete we are without them.

How much human compatibility is necessary for Christian community?—or does Christian faith, hope and reverence create and release human compatibility? I think this is a matter of timing, a matter of discerning, reverencing and respecting the person. Everyone needs a nest. Everyone has to be hatched and some people take a longer time than others. Everyone needs a small group; we need to be a best friend to someone and we need to have a best friend. We need to have some very close friends. We know we are poor, that we cannot yet share ourselves equally with everyone. This is an ideal and perhaps some day we will reach it. There is a need of compatibility just as in the home we need one father and one mother in a close union. We reach out further beyond in the degree that the nest does its job; we become people able to go out and be with those who are different from us. When boys are growing up they have no desire to mix with girls and girls want nothing to do with boys at some stages of their development. When a certain point is reached the boy scouts become girl scouts and girl scouts become boy scouts. There are different times when one is more or less ready. Something is being said when some Christians say they have to have a humanly compatible community. This is understandable, provided that it does not become an end in itself, otherwise, it can become a crippling thing. It will become abortive and human nature takes care of it. Most of these communities do not last.

When people are too much alike they know every thought and word of the other on a superficial level. What often happens in that kind of closeness is that we condition one another, we manipulate one another; we limit the other so that he cannot be other than our expectation of him. Our perception determines his behavior. He is not free to be who he is. And then the really mature person leaves home. Some seek the "compatible community" because they never received the hatching they should have experienced earlier and they are still looking for it. Ideally, what a Christian is aiming at is that wherever he is, he is at home.

"Lord, that I may see. Increase my faith." We must be aware that there is a dark side within ourselves and that our words, thoughts and our dreams are so far ahead of our actions. We can gaze upon the mountains but we are not there. We can see them, because we are deep in the valley. We are in the springtime of community; we must constantly be planting, constantly weeding. We must be discerning and the man who attempts it by himself, is weakened because there is much of himself that he cannot see, that he cannot hear. We need the brotherhood, we need the fraternity, we need one another, not to accuse us, but that by sharing themselves with us, we may discern ourselves in their light. We need one another's light, one another's forgiveness, one another's healing.

The Holy Spirit is given to us as a consolation because we do not have the human Jesus whom we can touch and see and taste. The Holy Spirit is this kinship, this affinity. He is the love of God poured out upon us so we can recognize God as our Father and one another as belonging to each other. "Let us go on loving one another, for love comes from God . . ." and "Love your neighbor as yourself." Love is the answer to every one of the commandments. Love is the most difficult of all the virtues and, therefore, the last to be expected of us but it is *the* sign by which we proclaim we follow Christ. We are being called continually to establish community, to breathe community. No one can prevent us from growing in the holiness to which Christ calls us. No structure nor institution, nor anything else can hinder us in our love of Jesus. There is no fraternity without Jesus, and without fraternity there is no real sign of Jesus. Because community is never established completely we must call for that which we cannot do of ourselves—so that by the power of Jesus and His Spirit in us we may enter into the mystery of forgiveness, the mystery of understanding one another and truly loving one another. Slowly we will grow into the covenant brotherhood.

7 Fraternity

"For where two or three are gathered together in my name, there am I in the midst of them " Mt. 18, 20.

"I am longing to see you; I want to bring you some spiritual strength, and that will mean that I shall be strengthened by you, each of us helped by the other's faith " Rom. 1, 11.

"Your mind must be renewed by a spiritual revolution . . . You must speak the truth to one another, since we are all parts of one another . . . let your words be for the improvement of others as occasion offers, and do good to your listeners " Eph. 4, 23-29.

"Let the message of Christ, in all its richness, find a home with you. Teach each other, and advise each other in all wisdom " Col. 3, 16.

Some years ago, Romano Guardini expressed his conviction that a basic cause for diminishing faith is our inability or unwillingness to share our faith experiences with one another. Without this sharing, he believed individual faith is weakened. Fifty years later, in the midst of our present theological traumas, a spiritual evolution is happening in the emergence of small-group faith communities which I describe as fraternities.

What is a Fraternity?

A fraternity is as new and as ancient as this morning's liturgy. It is a fundamental Christian experience. The first fraternity was that begun by Christ in his calling together the Twelve. The fellowship and brotherhood (koinonia) of the early Christian communities were a fraternity experience. Today's fraternity continues that pattern. A group comes together to pray, to listen to the Word, to share, to be responsible for one another and to one another. Its members celebrate both the present mystery of their life in Christ and Christ's life in and through them in the world. In a deep sense, the fraternity lives out the Eucharist in the actuality of the ordinary things of life. Openess to Christ in the presence of one another develops a givenness to each other. This experience embodies the true meaning of co-responsibility which nourishes the grace and charism given to each for the service of all. Through a fraternity one grows in the capacity to see more and more in the light of faith and to draw and call each other to a more complete response to the Father. Fraternity is, simply stated, the actualizing and living-out our love for one another through the recognized presence of Jesus in our midst.

Why Fraternity?

We are caught in a time of great change in which familiar cultural patterns, customs, structures and guidelines have been swept away. "Crisis" is on everyone's tongue—crisis in faith, crisis in education, crisis in cities, crisis in marriage. "Crisis" is a good Greek word signifying judgment, discernment, decision. In that sense, life is a crisis! Because we are free, the human condition will always be in crisis. We are always in process of growth and development and its dialectic, caught in "over-choice" and "alternate eternities." We are polarized between anonymity and community; alienation and over-involvement; loneliness and people-suffocation.

In the paradox of our life today we need community, perhaps more intense community than ever. We need privacy, a solitude richer than we have ever experienced. Too much community stifles and depersonalizes; too much solitude begets a barren and sterile loneliness and alienation. Change generates new perceptions and fresh needs emerge. There are today new levels of self awareness, personal consciousness. There is the quest for inner freedom, for self-determination. There is resistance to authority, to structures, to systems. Personal relationships have displaced rules. The people you choose to be with become themselves the structure.

In times of transition and instability human institutions contract to basic primary units. There is too great a gap between the large community and close friendship and it is into this vacuum that fraternity has moved. It neither displaces or is a substitute for either because both are necessary. Rather it is a response to a new need, a new life situation.

Value of Fraternity

A fraternity offers an adult experience of a family. When we were young we could not wait to move out from our families. After we have left, we spend the rest of our lives seeking and developing a family of friends. This family of friends, a wall of friends, is a need, a human universal which no one ever outgrows. This is not only a human need but a personal right, guaranteed by the essence of the Christian experience. Fraternity is built upon the truth that we need an inner community of friends. A faith community is essential for balance, for maturity, for continuing growth. In this family of friends one can be wholly himself, loved not so much, or even, for what he does, but simply that he is.

Fraternity is built upon the truth that Christ willed men to be saved by men. We need one another. In fraternity we make our life in Christ visible before our brothers, asking them to hold us faithful to our call and to our grace. One of the great weaknesses in our faith life is that it remains too invisible, known only to God in that vertical I—Thou relationship. Fraternity enables that vertical relationship to touch the horizontal life where Christ must be made visible.

In my own experience, the first value of fraternity is to help me in fidelity. "How often have I seen myself in a mirror and walked away, forgetting what manner of man I am." The common sin is non-response to grace. It is not a matter of being bad, but it is plateauing year after year in a slowly contracting self-gravitational orbit. The grace of fraternity is to enable one to break out of that orbit and to be given that thrust which is impossible to attain alone.

Size of Fraternity

The size of a fraternity is conditioned by the psychological limits of relationship. No one can relate deeply to twenty people at the same time. The group range is generally from eight to twelve persons. There may be several fraternities in the same House. There is no compulsion to belong. Fraternity does not mean a clique. It stands rather for inclusion rather than for exclusion. There can be both diversity and spirit of unity. Everyone will benefit; those not in a fraternity will belong by affinity.

Growth in Fraternity

Week after week one becomes aware of the effort another is making and the prayer he is living. Each one sees another in his struggle and becomes aware that when he fails he is in some way allowing the others to fail. No one's faith can be lived in isolation. What one does affects all. Fraternity brings home with unassailable impact that we are brothers and are entrusted with ultimate responsibility for each other. I deeply know that as I go, so they go; as they go, so go I. Growth in a faith community is growing together in Christ through one another.

Review of Life

The dynamic of a fraternity is called a review of life. Every fraternity meeting is like the meeting on the road to Emmaus. Like the disciples we are "deep in conversation about everything that has happened. And while they were absorbed in their serious talk and discussion, Jesus himself approached and walked along with them." Like the disciples, "The Scriptures are made plain to us" and "all that has happened" takes its right place in God's plan. "Our eyes are opened and we recognize Jesus walking beside us, when He broke bread."

The review of life rests on a fundamental fact: God acts through the events or at least through certain events and experiences of our life to become present to us, to manifest his love and bring us to renew and deepen our union with him.

The review of life helps us to discover the presence of Jesus and his expectations of us in all aspects of our life. It develops our fraternal openness and brings us to a more total giving of ourselves to God. Each member becomes the responsibility of the others. It forms in us the habit of seeing everything in the light of faith and draws us to a fuller response to the will of our Father.

The review of life is not an examination of conscience. Essentially it is an effort to look together at our life and to what Jesus is calling us. We are taught by our daily events and experiences if we "review" them with faith. This is why the review of life must start from *precise facts* drawn from our actual day and week.

To be effective, the fraternity review of life is preceded by an hour of prayer during which each member reviews his own week or month in order to recognize how Christ has acted in him and how he has responded. Each prays for discernment to speak and to listen to Christ in the presence of one another.

Usually it is difficult to recognize a *fact* of one's life, accustomed as we are to speak of ideas and thoughts and opinions. We are used to speaking in terms of "they," and "we," and "you." In contrast, the review of life is in the first person singular, forcing one to confront the facts and habits of one's daily life. One can always be more objective about others than about oneself.

The review of life comes no more easily than deep self-knowledge. It is a slow and stumbling process with no step-by-step guide. In every review of life, every fraternity is the uniqueness of its members.

Life growth and personal growth are rarely obvious. Paul's epistles often became a review of life.

Dynamics of the Review

As a general rule, a review of life begins with each one expressing a particular fact of one's week. "I feel I have been neglecting personal prayer." "I'm avoiding this person." "I have a new understanding of forgiveness through this happening this week." Or one might ask a question "What made this week for you?" "What do you feel you are to share?" "What of your week brought a new light on the Gospel or what demands were made on you?" "What decisions are you facing?" "How are you following through on your commitments?" In these ways, we come to each other with our needs, sharing our bread and asking for bread. We gradually come to ask one another "Teach me your prayer, your fidelity, your poverty, your love." "Share with me your Jesus." In some meetings there might not be any fact, experience or grace to share. One might not be ready to express what is developing or happening. No one is to feel any pressure to share. No one responds to what another has said except at the invitation of that person.

In essence, then, a review of life is primarily a prayer experience, an experience of Jesus and of oneself before Him and in Him. As we have said, no fraternity with one another is possible unless it is rooted in fraternity with Jesus. Only through His presence can we enter into the deeper presence of one another. In the review, we ask Jesus to help us to discern His presence in us, to reveal what He is calling us to and how to share Him with the fraternity. New levels of faith and charity emerge. A new sense of His presence is recognized in the way others express what it is for them to be with Jesus. One learns to discern what the Word is saying in this situation and to be sensitive to the Word. Since fraternity means reverence, a deep reverence for the mystery and secret that another person is and Who it is that is at work in each, psychological or moralistic probing has no place in the review of life. Each person is respected for the inner rhythm of this life in the Spirit. No one may decide, "This is the hour. Now is the moment of grace," or "I have the answer to your problem." Although we are called to be ministers of grace to each other, it cannot come precipitously, brashly, or insensitively. It is a beautiful experience to watch the unfolding of the unknown grace in each other as we search together to live our life according to the Gospel. It is important to "call" one another, to hear another's expectation of me and for them to hear my expectation of them, their need of me and mine of them.

In many ways the fraternity review of life is a living out, an actualization of the sacramental reality of the Eucharist and Penance. The effect of the Eucharist is to bond us to one another to enable us to hear Jesus deep within us always uttering his transforming words over each person in every situation of our life "This is my body; This is my blood."

The presence of Jesus in us makes us "an altogether new creature " Gal. 6, 16. He enables us in a new way to relate to others. His presence enables us to experience a new presence in others . . . "that each part may be equally concerned for all the others. If one part is hurt, all parts are hurt with it. If one part is given special honor, all parts enjoy it. Now you *together* are Christ's body; but each of you is a different part of it " I Cor. 12, 26-27. "If we live by the truth and in love, we shall grow in all ways into Christ, who is the head by whom the whole body is fitted and joined together, every joint adding its own strength, for each separate part to work according to its function. So the body grows until it has built itself up, in love " Eph. 4, 15-16.

Eucharist, the fraternity with Jesus, creates our capacity for fraternity with one another. He alone can free us from our inability to love as He loves us. Fraternity is the environment for penance, the sacrament of reconciliation, to reach a new fulness. For too long Eucharist and Penance have been contracted to the private individual sphere of I and Thou. So little of these sacraments is corporately and communally experienced. These sacraments give us power but rarely do we find an environment to actualize His grace in us for others. Many have left their life commitments not so much because they have been hurt by someone or by the community but because they have not been healed. The hungry continue to be sent away empty. Fraternity means healing, it is for giving—forgiving. We discover that we have a power in Christ to forgive sin, the offense against us. It is a real power, just as we have the power to bless, because of the reality of Christ's presence in us. We have real power even though it is not the sacerdotal power of absolution, it is a forgiveness through the power of understanding and compassion. We are peacemakers and joybringers because we express visibly Christ's person and Christ's forgiveness in love.

Fraternity and Review of Life is a risk. It is as dangerous as prayer—one never knows where He will lead. Fraternity and review of life is a contemporary way of responding to His Word. "By this love you have for one another, everyone will know that you are my disciples " Jo 13, 15. His words of judgment cannot but haunt us: "I know all about you: how you are neither cold nor hot. I wish you were one or the other, but since you are neither, but only lukewarm, I will spit you out of my mouth . . . I am the one who reproves and disciplines all those he loves; so repent in real earnest. Look, I am standing at the door, knocking. If one of you hears me calling and opens the door, I will come in to share his meal side by side with him . . . If anyone has ears to hear, let him listen to what the Spirit is saying to the churches!" Rev. 3, 15-22.

8

Your Jesus and My Jesus

"A Christ who is the power and wisdom of God."[1]

"He has become our wisdom, and our strength, and our holiness, and our freedom."[2]

+ + + + + + + + + + + + + +

"Who do people say I am?" . . . "But you," he asked, "who do you say I am?"[3] To the question Jesus asked his disciples, Peter responded for all of them, "You are the Christ, the Son of the living God."[4] What a rich addition to the gospels would have been given had each of the disciples answered His question. Each gospel is an answer by one evangelist from his individual experience and interpretation of the Christian community's faith. John's profile of the Word differs significantly from

Mark's vivid description of Jesus' acts of power-healing and exorcism. The Jesus Matthew reveals as the new Moses, the ultimate Teacher, has a perspective distinct from the Lukan account of the person-centered, loving-forgiving Jesus.

When the reader turns to Paul's writings, he finds only a rare reference to the public ministry of Jesus or to his words. His experience is of the risen Christ, the Christ who has identified Himself with Paul and with each Christian: "I live now, not with my own life but with the life of Christ who lives in me."[5] Christ did not ask Paul, "Who do you say I am?" Rather, it was Paul who asked, "Who are you?" and heard the answer, "I am Jesus whom you are persecuting."[6] From that moment, Paul could say, "I know Him in whom I believe."[7] More than any other apostle or evangelist, Paul gives intimate testimony to the meaning of Jesus for himself. "Life to me is Christ."[8] His exuberance is hardly containable: "I look on everything as so much rubbish if only I can have Christ and be given a place in him . . . All I want is to know Christ and the power of his resurrection and to share his sufferings by reproducing the pattern of his death . . . I am still running, trying to capture the prize for which Christ Jesus captured me."[9] He says emphatically, "There is only Christ, he is everything and he is in everything."[10] Later, in his letter to the Romans, Paul concludes that magnificent eighth chapter with the words: "I have become absolutely convinced that neither death nor life . . . nor anything else in God's whole world has any power to separate us from the love of God in Christ Jesus our Lord."[11] In the letter to the Hebrews, the focus is upon Christ as priest and mediator—"This one, because he remains forever, can never lose his priesthood. It follows, then, that his power to save is utterly certain, since he is living forever to intercede for all who come to God through him."[12] And the book of Revelation gives us the powerful figure of the one who cries out, "Look, I am standing at the door, knocking. If one of you hears me calling and opens the door, I will come in to share his meal, side by side with him."[13] Image upon image is convoked in this brilliant book. "I am the Alpha and the Omega, says the Lord God, who is, who was, and who is to come, the Almighty (Pantokrator)."[14] "I am the living One."[15] "Here is the message of the Amen, the faithful, the true witness, the ultimate source of God's creation."[16] The title "Amen" is rare but most significant. "Amen" comes from the same Hebrew root as the word "fidelity" and "truth." Christ is the perfect "Amen," witnessing both to the Church's fidelity to God and God's fidelity to the Church.

Christ is indeed the ultimate "Amen." Because this is true, man will never be able to put a final Amen to the inexhaustable mystery of Jesus. There is no word for the

Word. Even as man makes the attempt, he discovers that words and images conceal as much as they reveal. The Mosaic law rightly forbade images; they tended to shadow rather than to enlighten. Words, figures, images, symbols are finite, each with a life span and time limit—they die quickly. That there can never be a wholly encompassing conclusive word for Jesus is abundantly indicated in the New Testament. Jesus unfolds himself continuously before his disciples, depth upon depth, mystery upon mystery. Perspectives, dimensions, facets multiply; Jesus, Christ, Prophet, Teacher, Son of Man, Shepherd, Servant, Prophet, Son of God, Priest, Lord, Word. Each event, each action, each word opens new horizons. "I am the Living One"—yesterday and today, tomorrow and forever. As history unfolds new capacities in man, new intuitions emerge. The Christian of the twentieth century sees Christ and is conscious of Him in ways not possible for any previous generation. He is the "Lord of History," the "Cosmic Christ," "Lord of the Absurd," "Lord of the Statistical Improbability." Biographies, images, icons of Christ continue beyond numbering. That is good. God has made us to his own image; we cannot but look for Him in ourselves.

For each of us, this expanding concept, this newness of Christ for our generation is filled with meaning. No one of us is all of Christ; we each bear but a small fragment, yet that fragment is immensely valuable because He made it. Each of us is a "living out" of what we can of His life which He mysteriously continues in us. "I am the vine, you are the branches . . . cut off from me you can do nothing."[17] "Now this Lord is the Spirit, and where the Spirit of the Lord is, there is freedom. And we, with our unveiled faces reflecting like mirrors the brightness of the Lord, all grow brighter and brighter as we are turned into the image that we reflect."[18]

The question, "Who is Jesus?" is today —as throughout the centuries—repeated with an insistence not to be evaded. Like the Pilate of "Superstar," there are so many "dying to be shown that you are not just any man." Two years ago the Secretary-General of the communist party in France became a Christian because, in his words, "Christ is not dead. I saw him in the street today." While not many can claim so dramatic an experience, our own experience, our own history of Jesus is none-the-less real. "Who is He?" is not asked in terms of theology or scripture or anthropology but in terms of who is He to each of us! What is our life-experience of Jesus? I would say in answer to Him: "You know me! I have spent more time with you than with anyone else in the world! You are my other self, my consciousness of value and meaning. You have been with me. You have watched me grow from the moment of my conception through every one of your years in me, every one of your experiences. How you must have enjoyed yourself in me until now I am older than you were." Yet how much have I not experienced! Being in Jesus!—To experience Him as within, to experience his presence in others is to begin to understand.

What is this cumulative experience of Him in me, through people, His Word, Sacraments, prayer and life? How sad it is to experience so much and remember so little! It is "like looking at your own features in a mirror and then after a quick look, going off and immediately forgetting what you looked like."[19] It is startling to recognize how much each of us can be out of touch with his own life and history. It might be well for us to write our own Gospel like Luke; "after carefully going over the whole story from the beginning, I have decided to write an ordered account."[20] What is your infancy narrative, your first conscious awareness of Jesus? Perhaps the crib at Christmas time, a picture, statue or crucifix in your home; the visits to Church, First Communion. Who have been the Christ-figures in your life? It is always difficult for those baptized as infants to say what difference Christ has made in life, for there has never been a moment when Christ has not been in their lives.

Yet there are certain moments of light, peak experiences, intensified consciousness, times of crisis and decision. In dark periods He may break into our lives; He is there—in our joy or sorrow or glory. Where have you found Him; where has He found you? Jesus says, "My Father goes on working and so do I."[21] "I have made your name known to them and will continue to make it known."[22] Each of us is under command to witness to His life in us. If we are ashamed of Him before men, He will be ashamed of us before His Father in heaven. Each is called to remember and ponder Him in our hearts and to celebrate His presence. He is in our life, the whole of it. Each of us is different because of his entry and presence in our life. Again and again He calls us to "come" and to rest with Him in prayer. Then He compels us to "go" in ministry and service in his name to others. It is important to recognize how Jesus speaks to us in the events of our everyday. To each of us he gives a gift of himself to celebrate and share with others; as we grow, so He grows. As there is a "new" to us, so there is a "new" to Him. The ancient truth of Christ is ever new, because truth is always new and fresh, alive and living. He will always be "news," and Good News at that. Our Jesus of yesterday is not the Jesus of today as the mustard seed of yesterday is not the bush of today. We come to new consciousness, new intuition, new knowledge, new words, new languages. To come to know another person is an immense journey. Jesus is an immense journey that each of us must travel from the infant at Bethlehem to the Risen Christ enthroned in glory at the right hand of His Father.

There is a hunger for Jesus today, often unconscious but becoming more and more explicit. Our contemporary psalms, the popular songs, folk music and now rock music keep asking those "questions": "What's it all about, Alfie?" "Is this all there is to the circus?" "Does anyone know what time it is? Does anyone really care?" Something has happened to all of us. A whole culture continues to go through a new type of inward looking. Mass media seems to foster an around-the-world-anxiety. We experience a depth of loneliness that perhaps no people ever before experienced. I don't think that any people have ever been as lonely or experienced more alienation, powerlessness and willlessness than we have. Yet perhaps never before have people experienced so much oneness, concern, and possibility for community. Maybe the reality is the same but the possibility and capability of articulating and expressing ourselves is distinctively new. Today we have increasingly an ability to talk about the deep-down-things that no one else has ever heard us speak about, about what is the "really-real." We have a different way of thinking of ourselves. We experience ourselves in ways that have not happened before. We look to the roots, where we have come from. We return to Scripture and often we are startled at what we find there. He is not just metaphors, not mere figures of speech. We do not simply imitate Christ or follow Christ at a distance. We overtake Him or rather He takes over us. He grasps hold of me! Something really happens. Christ is not just an idea, a thought, a mentality. There is a realness, an utterly real reality to Him, as real as our own life.

We search into the depths of ourselves because at least there we are sure of something. We touch that which we can call the ground of our being. We experience an "isness" to life, an "I-am-ness." We can in some way intuit a presence to ourselves not before experienced. We cannot wholly account for it. We seem to be operating out of new resources within ourselves, some new kind of intuition and higher perception. There is a sense of meaning, a sense of mystery, a sense of aloneness in depth. So much can be experienced in a single day that it is difficult to recognize most of these perceptions and intuitions. Perhaps it springs from new leisure, perhaps from new exposures. There is an acceleration to our life that man has not before known. We search for a meaning to this new consciousness. No one is satisfied with being only a happening, merely being there. Scripture has begun to speak to us again. The Word of God sets off vibrations in us, new resonances. It rings true to our explorations. Something and someone has preceded us, and He continues and we continue. Wherever we stand, we have to stand on faith, consciously or fatalistically. Atheism is the vacuum of faith. Humanism is a faith forgotten. So we are going to stand in faith, a faith that demands a radical decision. We have to choose. We cannot choose whether we are going to die or not, but we can choose with whom to die, for what to die, and where to die. As long as we carry the name Christian with faith, we affirm a unique meaning to our life that has been validated for two thousand years. Its history has all the horrendous failings that have hampered all men. Yet it has a dream that seems to fulfill the deepest desires and intuitions of man's heart and spirit. "Where else can we go?" Choosing to die in the Christian community determines the way we live.

The awakened consciousness of being, to be in Christ, gives us a capacity to do what we would never dare without Him. There is a power, a strength, a wisdom, a freedom, a Person who really lives in us, activates us, who is our life on the deepest and fullest level. It is an experience as new and as old as the Incarnation. Christ continues the Incarnation in us, making us men for all men, men for God. Yet we must remember that Christ makes the ultimate difference to our lives only if his love, his truth touches us at the deepest level. The totality of human history is the continuing encounter with Christ. Perhaps the most beautiful, meaningful words of the Resurrection are, "He is not here . . . Now He is going before you to Galilee; it is there you will see him."[23] Wherever we go, He will be there ahead of us. We are the ones who must catch up.

Christ is the Alpha and the Omega, the first man, the ultimate man, the totality of what man will ever come to be. Christ possessed His humanity in a far fuller way than any man of his time or of our time. We possess ours only so far as humanity is developed up to our time. Christ possessed humanity as it is to evolve to the end of time. He is the whole man. What an embarrassment Christ is to us! He refuses to fit into our categories, into our new knowledge, our new theologies. There is always an element beyond where we have arrived. We can hold only so much of Him at any one time. Sometimes it is only His divinity; sometimes, as in our day, it is only His humanity. The theologian can no more contain Christ in his theology than the child hold the earth in his hand. Who can understand the elusive and ineffable truth. "All things were created through Him and for Him. Before anything was created, He existed and He holds all things in unity . . . because God wanted all perfection (pleroma) to be found in Him and all things to be reconciled through Him and for Him, everything in heaven and everything on earth."[24] The entire cosmos is filled with His creative presence. Christ is "out there" ahead of us, approaching us out of the future, coming toward us from the end of time. He is the beyond in the midst of our life, the future becoming present. Discovering Him is like opening boxes within boxes, secrets within secrets, mysteries within mysteries but in reverse. One opens a little box only to find a bigger box, a bigger world, a greater universe!

The Transfiguration continues. Each of us is given moments of His transparency and we cry out, "It is the Lord." He promised to manifest Himself, to show Himself, to draw us to Himself. All the images of Jesus are sacred. Each moment of the incarnation is an epiphany, has an eternal, inexhaustible dimension to which we must be open. The cosmic Christ is not only the pre-existent Christ, but also the One who carries forever the only thing in heaven made by the hands of man—the wounds of Calvary.

The cosmic Christ speaks to some; the Christ of e. e. cummings speaks to others:

> no time ago
> or else a life
> walking in the dark
> i met christ jesus
>
> my heart
> flopped over
> and lay still
> while he passed
>
> as close as i'm to you
> yes closer
> made of nothing
> except of loneliness

Christ alone—single-handed—taking on the sin, evil, absurdity and chaos of all men!

How did He dare? No man could, only God would—so only could "the love of one man compensate for the hatred of millions." Christ was poorer than the poorest. He never enjoyed anything that was beyond the reach of the least of his brethren. He had nothing for Himself that another could use. Waking in the morning, He experienced the discouragement of the masses of people. He knew anger, love, fear, frustrations. It is not surprising some poet wrote that more amazing than his miracles were His tears.

Still Jesus remains a stumbling block; His foolishness still remains, especially regarding the reality of sin, "that Jesus Christ came into the world to save sinners" and I myself am the greatest of them.[25] For us He became sin. Why? Suffering for sin? There are so few totally deliberate sins, so few who know, who understand. Suffering is the visible presence of sin or of healing, and Christ wanted to be with sinners in their depth of agony and loneliness. He suffered so much because men are suffering and so that in Him each could recognize himself—Christ in the breadline, Christ in prison, Christ in the morgue!

There is an absorbing question in theology today about the human consciousness of Christ. When did Christ in His human developing consciousness know that He was God? Imagine a man discovering that He is God! Yet what does all our theology of Christ point to? Imitating Christ, following

Him, union with Him, being taken up with Him, being taken in by Him? Or putting on Christ, ingrafted into Him, being the body of Christ, in, with, through Him?

"In the face of all this, what is there left to say?"[26] Christ is greater than His sacraments. The Word, the Sacraments, even the Incarnation is a kenosis, an emptying out, the poverty of Christ so that we may meet Him. Yet the Incarnation ultimately reaches its fulfillment in us become His Sacrament, until finally when we are asked "Who is Jesus?" with utmost faith and truth we can say, "I am Jesus."

1 I Cor. 1:25
2 I Cor. 1:31
3 Mk. 8:27
4 Mt. 16:16
5 Gal. 2:20
6 Acts 8:5
7 2 Tim. 1:12
8 Phil. 1:21
9 Phil. 3:8
10 Col. 3:11
11 Romans 8:38
12 Heb. 7:24
13 Rev. 3:20
14 Rev. 1:8
15 Rev. 1:18
16 Rev. 3:14
17 John 15:5
18 2 Cor. 4:18
19 James 1:23
20 Luke 1:4
21 John 5:18
22 John 17:26
23 Mt 28:6
24 Col. 1:16-20
25 1 Tim. 1:5
26 Romans 8, 31

9

Mary and Joseph

To remember Jesus is to remember those closest to Him. Christian people have instinctively and tenaciously hallowed the memory of Mary and Joseph. Popular devotion may wane but with the persistence of the ocean tides, the humble figures of Christ's parents rise again and again into Christian consciousness. As the humanity of Jesus becomes more and more central, so does the humaness of Mary and Joseph.

So little of them is known, so much more would we like to know. Their hiddenness yet reknown continues to draw the Christian imagination and heart. They are a mystery yet have a universality that embraces every generation, every culture. Everone of the faithful has his own special image and favorite title for them. Every Christian senses a kinship, a relationship with them that clothes him with an identity and a dignity. To be a disciple of Jesus is to receive Mary and to be of her is to be related to Joseph.

The Christian will never "get over" the mystery that a woman has given birth to God. The human mind is still stunned and will be until time shall be no more. To be Christian is to live with an undiminishable sense of astonishment, awe and wonder as one prays the first prayer of the New Testament, the prayer of the Incarnation, the Hail Mary. "The Lord is with you" "The Holy Spirit will come upon you" "Let what you have said be done to me".

What must have been Mary's celebration of the first moment of the Incarnation, of redemption! It is not difficult to appreciate the beautiful truth of Mary's own conception, that the effects of her son's life were realized in her from the first moment of her existence. The decisive moment of God's evolutionary call to man was not unprepared—she had won God's favor, she was full of grace. Incomprehensible, yet how right and fitting! God does such things!

In the beginning God spoke a word to Adam but he did not listen. When God spoke his final word it was to a woman and through her listening, man came to know God as Abba, Father. It will always be the glory of women that the Good News was given to Mary first. Joseph was the second to know. What human and divine faith was called forth from Joseph and Mary. They were fully human, espoused, committed to each other, to marriage and family. What love must have existed between them! If one is to use superlatives, certainly Mary and Joseph were the world's greatest lovers! Was any man ever loved more than Joseph, or any women loved more than Mary? What understanding, compatibility and depth must have been theirs. Yet what anguish, incomprehension, what hidden sorrow in Mary's knowing Joseph's struggle to understand. How significant is Schillebeeckx's profound insight that the virginity of Mary and Joseph came into being through the annunciation of the Incarnation and did not predate it! What joy they must have shared when Joseph has his annunciation and the angel told him, "Joseph, son of David, do not be afraid to take Mary as your wife. What she has conceived is conceived of the Holy Spirit and she will give birth to a Son, whom you will call Jesus (the Savior) for it is He who will save His people from their sins. (Mt. 1:22). Joseph was a son of Abraham. What desire he must have had for a son of his own flesh. Now everything was changed. Imagine even the most dedicated young man and woman of today about to be married, and then suddenly to be called to live together virginally!

In the mystery of the Incarnation Christian virginity comes into being. It is a great mystery. A new capacity is given and called forth from man and woman. A new depth of relationship between man and woman becomes possible because Jesus thrusts his presence into their lives. Christian virginity is born with and in the mystery of Jesus. It shares in his impenetrableness. It will be no more humanly understood than he is. It has always been "un-understood," much misunderstood and often distorted. Today it is an embarrassing confrontation, as is every truth of the Gospel. One cannot remain neutral before truth. It demands response or repression. Virginity is the suffering servant of Jesus. It has no meaning or value except as an incarnation of His presence.

How we wish Joseph had left a journal that we might know how he worked out his call! It really was not optional. Like truth, grace and call are free but not optional. The mystery of virginity is that it can be the expression of the deepest reality of human love and a sign of the love in the life to come when there will be neither giving or receiving in marriage.

What must have been Mary's presence to Joseph and Joseph's to Mary! What must have been their beautiful path of becoming ever more one in Spirit. They had to go through every stage of growth, development and understanding. How they must have grown through Jesus and be born through the child. In their virginity, Joseph was truly the husband of Mary and Mary was truly wife. How long did it take them to grow into being husband and wife? How long did it take them to become father and mother?

What words and what silence they shared as they contemplated the mystery of what lay ahead for this child. How often they were torn out of their home and walking the roads—to Bethlehem, to Egypt, to Nazareth, to Jerusalem. How well Jesus learned their prayer "fiat"—your will be done! No one ever had to respond with greater faith and live in greater darkness than Mary and Joseph. They were the darkness before dawn, waiting for the deep light slowly to unfold in ever richer depth and intensity, from magnitude to magnitude, from magnificat to magnificat.

What was the father-son relationship of Joseph and Jesus? Joseph is truly the father of Jesus for Jesus had to learn his manhood from Joseph. His personality, strength and character grew through Joseph and Joseph grew through Jesus. From him Jesus learned to work in stone and wood and to be a man among men. What does a father share with his son, a son with his father? Humanly Jesus came to know God as Father through experiencing Joseph as father, one fatherhood intensifying and enlightening the other. In the way every child does Jesus came to know Mary through Joseph and Joseph through Mary and himself through both. What must have been their morning and evening prayer together! What must have been their Passover celebration when Jesus would ask the question "What does this ritual mean" (Ex 12, 27). How were those Sabbaths in the Synagogue of Nazareth where Jesus would one day announce that the prophecy of Isaias was fulfilled before them in himself! When did Joseph first walk with him to Tabor which dominates the eastern horizon from the edge of Nazareth?

The life of Mary and Joseph is unknown, hidden, perhaps so that we can come to understand it through the unfolding of the undramatic mysteries of our own life, to be understood only by prayerful living. Their life like ours is one of hidden fidelity, secret service, being man, woman, neighbor, friend, worker, father, mother, husband, wife. Mary and Joseph are the light and dignity of everyday life. How beautiful the title, "Madonna of the Broom." What did Mary do when her neighbor dropped in as she was sweeping the floor? What did they talk about? Perhaps it was about her bread in the oven, the cloth she was mending, the work of Joseph, the laughter of Jesus! Mary and Joseph call every Christian into an intimacy with Jesus and an ever deepening consciousness of the little people and things of life. Mary was Jesus' gift to us from the Cross. Each of us is to recognize something of her living in us. Each of us is an annunciation that Jesus is here; a visitation that makes another person leap for joy; a new birth of life each day; a presentation, a consecration to Him we have learned to know as Father; a finding, a discovery of Him who is at work in us. "From generation to generation all shall call me blessed." What must have been the prayer of Mary with the Apostles. What must have been the meaning of the Eucharist which Mary celebrated with John as she prayed the words of consecration, "This is my body, this is my blood." Mary's last recorded words in Scripture were "Do whatever he tells you." He awaits our fiat, our yes so that again He can work the miracle of Cana, the compassion of Calvary, the Pentecostal fire of the upper room.

10

Letter from Assekrem

Friday, May 28, 1971
Assekrem, Sahara

"Be happy at all times; pray constantly; for all things give thanks to God, because this is what God expects you to do in Christ Jesus " (I Thess. 5:17)

Dear fellows,

May the Holy Spirit scorch each and everyone of you where you most need to be scorched this Pentecost! Many of you will probably be on the road this Memorial Weekend and I wish you great weather and safety.

It is 10:00 a.m. here as I write to you and that would make it 4:00 a.m. Michigan time. I am sitting at a makeshift desk in a stone and clay hermitage, five by ten feet, built inside the rim of a valley overlooking the desolate beauty of the Hoggar mountains and out of my door which opens directly into the sunrise I have a vista that is unbroken for two hundred miles! Assekrem is the center of the mountains of the Sahara desert and the Hermitage is at an elevation of almost nine thousand feet! This is certainly one of the most inaccessible places in the world today—imagine what it must have been sixty years ago when Foucauld first built his hermitage here! The utter desolation, barrenness, and starkness of these mountains defy description. I have seen nothing like them in the U.S., Europe, or Asia. The only resemblance I can suggest are some of those close-up shots of the surface of the moon. This is where the Tuareg people live, the nomads of the mountains and the desert, following a pattern of life which has varied little over the past ten thousand years. This is where Charles de Foucauld, the "universal brother," came to live in 1901 and among whom he was killed in 1916 at Tamanrasset, a three day camel ride from Assekrem.

You may well wonder what I am doing here, and there have been a few times these past three weeks that I have wondered myself! Last fall when it was definite that we would have a free May, I became conscious that the double sabbatical of my priesthood (fourteen years) and my fortieth birthday were coming up this year and that this would be an ideal time for a thirty-day retreat. So I did not accept any invitations to give retreats, workshops, etc. for this month and left it to the Lord to let his providence suggest where I should go. It came to the end of April and I still had nothing definite, but a very attractive invitation had been offered to spend the month with a priest hermit on Cat Island in the Bahamas. I had almost decided on that until Tuesday evening, April 27, when a long time lay friend of mine jokingly said, "Why don't you go to the desert where Foucauld finished out his life?" I laughed at the thought, but it wouldn't go away. The next afternoon I found myself checking the possibilities and they were slight, but somehow all the difficulties faded and before I fully realized it, I was in Tamanrasset, 1600 miles into the desert—without even a match, flashlight, bedding, knife, medicine, or cooking skills and to top it off—no hat!

It had taken almost nine hours to fly from Algiers to Tamanrasset, with four stops on the way. The vastness of the Sahara is hard and exhausting even to the imagination. Three Little Brothers live and work in Tamanrasset which has a population of three or four thousand and is the last settlement before Niger some eight hundred miles further south. I decided to forego the luxury of a three day camel trip to Assekrem, 80 kilometers away, and the

Little Brothers arranged for transportation by landrover which did it in six hours. The road brings you only to the foot of Assekrem, the last two thousand feet, 60° incline, is by goat trail! Providentially, Brother Roger from the Detroit Little Brothers, who has been on his year in the desert since last September, had arrived just a few hours before I did and met me half way up the mountain. I was never happier to see anyone!

Father Foucauld's Hermitage is a Chapel now and two Little Brothers are here permanently to carry on his work with the Tuaregs. Here is where the Little Brothers come to make their forty days in solitude. There are four or five small hermitages built far apart from each other on this vast plateau on the top of this mountain of Assekrem. They gave me the Hermitage in Valle' Tranquille about a mile directly north of Father Foucauld's Hermitage. My hermitage is utterly simple—an army cot, a table, a single burner with bottle gas and a lamp. A Chapel is built along side my hermitage, five by eight feet. A rain barrel lower on the hill is my source of water. And there I was in my own little hermitage on top of a mountain in the middle of the Sahara desert all by myself for the next three weeks!

The reality-shock came quickly. I was to survive on the desert diet—no meat, vegetables, fruit! My stables were bread, cheese, potatoes, rice, macaroni, tuna and sardines and dried dates! Readily I understood how Foucauld would spend only a half hour on all three meals a day!

Yet here it is three weeks later, and I can't say that I have ever been hungry, though I am sure I have lost four inches. I've enjoyed not shaving and I am almost used to not washing or changing my clothes. I have that Fidel Castro look now!

This has been a much longer introduction than I had intended. I want to share with you some of my thoughts and experiences of these weeks. In regards to reading material, "all" I brought was the Jerusalem Bible, the Jerome Biblical Commentary (believe it or not) and an old classic on "Interior Prayer" by Poulain, plus my notebook.

The sun rose right in my door way each morning at 5:00 a.m. I usually got up and blinked my eyes at it and then went back to "horizontal" meditation til seven. My breakfast was usually toast and tea—toast on the open fire. I tried powdered eggs once but that was enough. From 8-10 I spent in Chapel in prayer and reflection on the Psalms, Paul's Letters or John's Gospel.

10-2	Study of Scripture and reading Poulain or Commentary.
12-2	Lunch and Siesta and Walk if heat was not too intense
2-4	Study
4-5	Hour of Adoration
5-6	Eucharist. Usually another

priest and I concelebrated each day
6-7:30   Supper and leisure
7:30-9:30   Study, Reading, Writing

As I was leaving Detroit, different people asked me what I thought I would get out of it. "What will you bring back?" All I could answer was that I hoped to bring back a little more of Jesus and a little bit more of myself. I have been praying Foucauld's Act of Abandonment for eight years; now seemed a time to act on it and trust myself to His providence. If there was anything specifically I was seeking, it probably would be expressed in terms of a deeper interior grace of prayer and a more physical experience of poverty. Someone added, "Why go there?" and I answered without reflection, "Maybe just to discover that it isn't there."

Nothing extraordinary or dramatic has happened to me or taken place in me during these days or weeks, and yet something has. Maybe it has been the opportunity to be quiet and disengaged. Whatever it has been, it is very filling and very freeing. I remember some of the fear I had those first days, a kind of isolation-anxiety from the absence of the proximity and security of others; a fear of the unknown—intruders, animals, poisonous insects, unfamiliar food, water, etc.; then growing into a trust and a new sense of him whom I call "Father," who brought me into being and has carried me through to this day.

And in overcoming the fear there is born an exhiliarating kind of freedom and life. You become very simple, the complexities and fears fall away. You simply live the day, not fret, worry and think about it.

What has happened to me in the desert? The one clear thought that has come to me is that I have' absorbed a vast silence from the desert. Not a silence of emptiness but of fullness—pleroma, not kenosis—a silence that is a peace and communion and freedom.

After writing that, I came across something similar in John of the Cross: "the tranquility of solitude in which the soul is moved and guided to find things by the Spirit of God." Merton in commenting on this writes: "in this tranquil attention to God, God acts directly upon the one who prays, doing it Himself, communicating Himself to the soul, without other means, without passing through men, images, or forms . . . mysterious call to a life of direct communion with and dependence upon and guidance by and formation by and purification by God in silence, in prayer, in solitude, in detachment, in freedom."

One of the first probes into Scripture was the meaning of the desert. The Spirit drove our Lord into the desert and he remained there for forty days. Paul after his conversion writes "but I went off to Arabia at once " (Gal. 1:17). The commentators suggest that this was to parallel Jesus' desert experience or perhaps he went on pilgrimage to Sinai.

In Genesis 2:8 Paradise is pictured as an oasis in the eastern desert. Amos, Hosea, and Jeremiah regard the period in the desert as a time of perfect union between Yahweh and his people (Hosea 2:16). "That is why I am going to lure her out and lead her out into the desert and speak to her heart " (Jeremiah 31:2). "They have found pardon in the desert." It is the place of conversion which is the theme of second Exodus, from Babylon to Jerusalem. It was on the mountain in the desert that God spoke to Elijah, not in the mighty wind, not in the earthquake, nor in the fire, but in the sound of a gentle breeze (KK. 19). To go to the desert is to return to the source. There is always need of a new Exodus, the way of purification and conversion.

I found the desert a test, a challenge to faith and providence, a self-confrontation, with haunting words, "Can you drink the cup I have drunk?"—to be poor, to live on subsistence, to walk the edge of survival, to have no other resources except yourself and ME?"

As the quiet of the desert began to sink into me and I experienced the total freedom from all the things I am so busy about, I began to realize how much of an abandonment of God had taken place in my life. How easily "I had fled him down the nights and down the days and the arches of the years, lest having Him I might have nought else besides."

I noticed my games of avoidance and aversion from God lest further conversion cost too much. It is so easy to let the fire die out with just a little neglect and omission. I have become expert at staying on the horizontal, avoiding the vertical, skirting the cross, mortification, and discipline. I prayed: "Lord, where were you when I led myself into sin? Why do you let me forget you so often and wander in amnesia? Lord, how I refuse to recognize temptation! How easily I turn to myself and away from You. Your will is so readily ignored and avoided and my will so instantaneously followed. I hear myself praying, 'hallowed be my name, my kingdom come, my will be done.' Lord, it is only as a sinner that I can stand before you. I have taken to myself what belongs only to you. I cannot expect love, I do cry out for Mercy!

Another Scriptural theme that fascinated me was that of the Mountain—Sinai (Horeb), Zion (Sion). The mountains are God's favorite place of meeting with his people—Sinai, Nebo, Ebal, Gerizim, Zion, Carmel, etc. They are changeless witnesses, often personified. Zion (Jerusalem) eventually becomes the symbol of God's chosen people. It is the home of Jahweh and of his Anointed, the future meeting place of all the nations. With the vision of the new Jerusalem (Is. 54:11), the Bible closes Rev. 21. In Gen., 17:1 God first reveals his name to Abraham, "I am El Shaddai," i.e.,

Mountain God. Ps. 48 is the psalm of Zion, the mountain of God. In Micah 4, "In the days to come the mountain of the Temple of Jahweh will be put on top of the mountains and be lifted higher than the hills."

In Matthew's Gospel, the mountain is his favorite place: Mountain of temptation 4:8, mountain of the sermon 5:1, mountainside of the multiplication of the loaves 15:29, mountain of the transfiguration 17:1, and in 28:16 "meanwhile the eleven disciples set out for Galilee, to the mountain where Jesus had arranged to meet them." There he gave them their mission to the whole world.

The mountains are wrapped in silence, they are faithful witnesses in their changelessness. They are the place of great vista and vision. Difficult of access, courage and strength is demanded. In the very process of climbing, one discovers strength that he did not possess as he began. In mastering a mountain one absorbs the power of that mountain. Mountains are the sacramentals of God. Calvary is a mountain. The cross is the crown of aloneness on the mountain. The priest is a mountain climber, a God-seeker. His altar is a mountain.

How beautiful it was to celebrate Ascension on the mountain of Assekrem! I wanted to concelebrate the Liturgy with the Little Brothers, so I rose at dawn and walked up to Foucauld's Hermitage at 5:00 a.m. for the Mass at 5:15. Because of some expected visitors the Mass time was changed to 12:00 so I had seven hours of prayer before Mass! I meditated much on the mystery of His ascension that morning and on the fact that one of these days my person must ascend to our Father too. I thought of my very prayer being a little ascension of myself to the Father. I thought of the eleven in Matthew on that mountain in Galilee and I could almost hear them say to Jesus, "Lord, don't go! Don't leave us. We want You to stay with us, we want to be with You." But He "was taken up into heaven: there at the right hand of God He took His place" (Mark 16). Ten days later they were to understand when they began to experience his promise, "You will receive power" (Acts 1:8).

He who descended into us has taken all of us into Himself and when He ascends, he creates the way for all of us to follow him and be with him forever! I don't think our minds will ever comprehend the depths of John 17 which the Liturgy has given us this week. "Father, may they be one in us, as you are in me and I am in you . . . I want those you have given me to be with me where I am . . . I have made your name known to them and *will continue to make* it known, so that the love with which you loved me may be in them, and so that I may be in them!" I have been specially struck with this rare passage from II Cor. 3:17-18 — "Now this Lord is the Spirit, and where the Spirit of the Lord is, there is freedom. And we, with our unveiled faces reflecting like mirrors the brightness of the Lord, all grow brighter and brighter as we are turned into the image that we reflect; this is the work of the Lord who is Spirit."

My prayer that morning was a prayer of exuberant, soaring gratitude for the presence of Jesus in the world, in myself. The effect of his death and resurrection given in baptism, renewed and deepened in each Eucharist is the power that lifts me up to the Father. "I thank you, Jesus, for the power of your priesthood in me drawing me ever to your holy mountain. I thank you for the daily transfusion of your body and blood into me and all mankind. I thank you for your Word that is as lasting and as real as these mountains and fills my mind and heart with courage and hope. I thank you for your Covenant that you have made with me and again and again renew with me through the love and faith of so many you have sent into my life. May this ascension day be a lifting up of all of life, of the world beyond the clouds of fears and anxieties that so often overcast us. May each of us be risen out of the shallow depths of ourselves and be given a taste of the peace and joy that comes from entering into your presence."

The nights are glorious in the desert! The stars are incredibly close. The moon was full the first night in the desert and never have I seen it linger longer in the heavens. At one end of the skies from my hermitage is the Big Dipper and at the other end is the Southern Cross, four stars pointing to the South. The first time I've seen it. The stars have a powerful fascination, they bring you to awe and then to reverence. I thought of the stars as God's veil, his curtain. Perhaps each star is but a reflection of his hidden presence on earth in his saints! It was a consoling thought and encouraging.

The world as sacrament of God. How easy to sense this in the desert Mountains. The world is the face of God and we crawl all over it not recognizing Him. Everything is a sacrament and revelation of His goodness, power, beauty, and tenderness. Every person is an unrecognized presence and fragment of Him. My own existence is an experience of His life, His truth, His love! How small one can feel before the immensity of nature and yet how significant, because one is conscious of it, can appreciate, understand, and love it!

"Always be eucharistoi" (Col. 3:15). I like this expression of Paul — always be eucharists, thankers of the Father. The Mass continues to take on deeper meaning for me. In a sense, all that I do the whole day is to celebrate Eucharist! The Mass is a moment beyond time, yet the deepest moment of time. It is the Incarnation, Death, Resurrection, Ascension, and Pentecost in this unique day, the Lord with us and for us. How easily I forget the power of his priesthood in me! As a man I always carry within me the power of giving human life. As a priest I carry within myself the power of giving Christ's life and forgiveness to life already born. How little this is valued today! My desire is to become more and more personal with him, to live more and more conscious of him who "has become our wisdom, our power, our holiness and our freedom" (Cor. 1:31). My need is to enter into the power of Christ, not the power of conquering the world, but the simple yet decisive "yes" to him and "no" to myself. "How little and poor I am and how immense and loving you are! How can you know me? My little drop of water in your cosmos of love and light, truth and beauty. Lord, you pick up my nothingness and sweep it up into the extravagance of yourself, my match-flame into your sun!"

Every morning I have been up for the sunrise before 5:00 a.m. I cannot get tired of it! There is a terrible beauty to witnessing the sun slowly being born out of the womb of the earth! How often have I been reminded of Chardin's "Mass on the World." The sun is the Eucharist and dawn is exposition. The day is the pleroma, the filling up of the entire universe with his light and love. And sunset is reposition. How good it is to be able to rise each morning for exposition and to kneel each evening for reposition!

Jesus is a hunger! I am more and more deeply aware of this truth. He is everyone's hunger, consciously or unconsciously. The radical crisis of our times is the crisis of personal love. Everyone deeply experiences the desire to be loved, accepted and understood. I know I have an intense desire to be loved, whether I am deserving to be loved or not! I have to be loved with a love that is full of mercy, of forgiveness. To be forgiven is to be loved without any reason. There is not too much human love that can reach so far and long enough. So the ancient-ever-new-cry for love, "Lord, have mercy, have mercy!" I am learning again to be a beggar, to kneel at the foot of the altar and to hold out my hands for his mercy.

It is startling to grow into an awareness that Christ is incarnated into your own flesh! It takes years and years for the anointing of ordination to filter down into the dark depths that you were not even aware of yourself! I may not have been aware of them, but I am sure they come as no surprise to him.

I have known something of Paul's certain conviction of the presence, love and forgiveness of Jesus. His presence is with me always, within and without. He is present as the air is present, as truth and love are present. He is life, light, truth, and grace. He is my peace, my forgiver, my friend. An intimate friendship is to love with the whole heart and to know that I am loved; and therefore I am a part of the other and whatever I do affects the other! To love Jesus is to be true to Him, to be faithful to Him for what He has entrusted to me, to be His presence to others and to

(N.L.C.)

(I.C.E.L.)

ENTRY ANTIPHON
Let my prayer reach you, Lord; listen to my request.

Let my prayer come before you, Lord; listen, and answer me.

COLLECT
Almighty, eternal God, in your mercy protect us from all that can harm us. Liberate our minds and our bodies from every hindrance so that we may be free to do your will. Through our Lord.
Amen.

God of power and mercy, protect us from all harm. Give us freedom of spirit and health in mind and body to do your work on earth. Through our Lord.

Amen.

FIRST READING: 1 Kings 17: 10-16

Elijah went off to Sidon. And when he reached the city gate, there was a widow gathering sticks; addressing her he said, "Please bring a little water in a vessel for me to drink." She was setting off to bring it when he called after her. "Please" he said "bring me a scrap of bread in your hand." "As the Lord your God lives," she replied "I have no baked bread, but only a handful of meal in a jar and a little oil in a jug; I am just gathering a stick or two to go and prepare this for myself and my son to eat, and then we shall die." But Elijah said to her, "Do not be afraid, go and do as you have said; but first make a little scone of it for me and bring it to me, and then make some for yourself and for your son: For thus the Lord speaks, the God of Israel:

'Jar of meal shall not be spent,
jug of oil shall not be emptied,
before the day when the Lord sends
rain on the face of the earth.' "

The woman went and did as Elijah told her and they ate the food, she, himself and her son. The jar of meal was not spent nor the jug of oil emptied, just as the Lord had foretold through Elijah.

This is the word of the Lord.
Thanks be to God.

RESPONSORIAL PSALM: Psalm 145

RESPONSE: **My soul, give praise to the Lord.**

1. It is the Lord who keeps faith for ever,
who is just to those who are oppressed.
It is he who gives bread to the hungry,
the Lord, who sets prisoners free. (R.)

2. It is the Lord who gives sight to the blind,
who raises up those who are bowed down.
It is the Lord who loves the just,
the Lord, who sets prisoners free. (R.)

3. He upholds the widow and orphan
but thwarts the path of the wicked.
The Lord will reign for ever,
Zion's God, from age to age. (R.)

SECOND READING: Hebrews 9: 24-28

It is not as though Christ had entered a man-made sanctuary which was only modelled on the real one; but it was heaven itself, so that he could appear in the actual presence of God on our behalf. And he does not have to offer himself again and again, like the high priest going into the sanctuary year after year with the blood that is not his own, or else he would have had to suffer over and over again since the world began.

Instead of that, he has made his appearance once and for all, now at the end of the last age, to do away with sin by sacrificing himself. Since men only die once, and after that comes judgement, so Christ, too, offers himself only once to take the faults of many on himself, and when he appears a second time, it will not be to deal with sin but to reward with salvation those who are waiting for him.

This is the word of the Lord.
Thanks be to God.

ALLELUIA
Alleluia, alleluia! Even if you have to die, says the Lord, keep faithful, and I will give you the crown of life. Alleluia!

GOSPEL: Mark 12: 38-44

In his teaching Jesus said, ''Beware of the scribes who like to walk about in long robes, to be greeted obsequiously in the market squares, to take the front seats in the synagogues and the places of honour at banquets; these are the men who swallow the property of widows, while making a show of lengthy prayers. The more severe will be the sentence they receive.''

He sat down opposite the treasury and watched the people putting money into the treasury, and many of the rich put in a great deal. A poor widow came and put in two small coins, the equivalent of a penny. Then he called his disciples and said to them, ''I tell you solemnly, this poor widow has put more in than all who have contributed to the treasury; for they have all put in money they had over, but she from the little she has had put in everything she possessed, all she had to live on.''

This is the Gospel of the Lord.
Praise to you, Lord Jesus Christ.

PRAYER OVER THE OFFERINGS

Be moved to pity, Lord, by this sacrifice we offer you. We celebrate it as a memorial of your Son's passion: grant that through our devotion we may receive the grace it contains. Through Christ our Lord.
Amen.

God of mercy, in this eucharist we proclaim the death of the Lord. Accept the gifts we present and help us follow him with love, for he is Lord for ever and ever.

Amen.

PREFACE *OF SUNDAYS OF THE YEAR III (or at priest's choice)*

It is indeed right and fitting, it is our duty and leads to our salvation, that we should praise you always and everywhere, Lord, holy Father, almighty and eternal God. When God himself came to redeem our mortal race, you made death itself the remedy for death, and so revealed the riches of your glory. The source of our doom became transformed into the source of our salvation, through Christ

Father, all-powerful and ever-living God, we do well always and everywhere to give you thanks. We see your infinite power in your loving plan of salvation. You came to our rescue by your power as God, but you wanted us to be saved by one like us. Man refused your friendship, but man himself was to restore it through Jesus Christ our Lord. Through him the angels of heaven offer their prayer of adoration as they who is our Lord. Through Christ the armies of Angels who rejoice in your presence for ever, praise and adore your majesty. Let our voices blend with theirs, we entreat you, as we joyfully proclaim:

Holy, holy, holy Lord...

rejoice in your presence for ever. May our voices be one with theirs in their triumphant hymn of praise:

Holy, holy, holy Lord...

COMMUNION ANTIPHON

The Lord is my shepherd; there is nothing I shall lack. He has made me lie down in green pastures, and beside refreshing streams he has led me.

The Lord is my shepherd; there is nothing I shall want. In green pastures he gives me rest, he leads me beside the waters of peace.

POST COMMUNION

We thank you, Lord, for your gift of the Bread of Heaven. You have filled our hearts with your Spirit: grant that this power may keep us singleminded in your service. Through Christ our Lord.

Amen.

Lord, we thank you for the nourishment you give us through your holy gift. Pour out your Spirit upon us and in the strength of this food from heaven keep us singleminded in your service. Through Christ our Lord.
Amen.

THE REDEMPTORIST MASS LEAFLET
Mass texts from the National Liturgical Commission translation, the Grail Psalter (by permission of The Grail, England, and W. Collins & Co. Ltd.), Bible readings are taken from the JERUSALEM BIBLE©1966, 1967, 1968 by Darton, Longman & Todd Ltd., and Doubleday and Company Inc. and are used by permission of the Publishers. Antiphons from the English translation of the Roman Missal Copyright© 1973, International Committee on English in the Liturgy, Inc. All rights reserved.
Redemptorist Publications, Alton, Hants.

do to them as He would do. He is my
freedom and He has given it to me in the
desert where I have and am nothing! "Do
you love Me?" He asks. "Are you faithful
to Me? By your works I shall know!"

Well! That's a much longer epistle than
I had intended. It became a kind of thanksgiving prayer for me. I now can see why I
was suddenly and almost reluctantly drawn
here. I came not to get some flood of
insights and grace but to offer and give
myself individually to Him

to give thanks for the grace and strength of
the Church in Detroit where I live out
my life

to do penance for my sins and neglect of
grace, to make reparation for the fail-
ures and weaknesses of the priesthood

to intercede for grace upon all you fellows,
seminarians, to nourish that gentle tug
of Christ you are experiencing to
follow Him with all of your life.

I must say a final word of thank you
for the Little Brothers of Jesus here. Their
peace, joy, and tranquility are a continuous
inspiration to me. They are such selfless
and ambitionless men. God alone is their
life. They mean it in total literalness when
they pray "Do with me what you will."
They are men with no expectations, therefore, they are men with no frustrations.
They work on a principle of sheer totality,
complete instruments for his will—willing
to be ordained or not ordained, to work in

a coal mine or sweep streets, to be in prison or in the desert. They are always seeking the humblest, most undistinguished place. How truly they live Foucauld's charism—to love Jesus totally and to love every person as Jesus loves them! "Act, pray, suffer—these are our methods . . . Our annihilation is the most powerful means we have to unite ourselves to Jesus and to save souls . . . Men turn to God by you loving them."

P.S. I should tell you about our hike into the mountains to visit the Little Sisters of Jesus who live as nomads and herd goats. It was the most distinctive highlight of the time here. Brother Roger, another priest, and I left at 2:00 Sunday afternoon, the 23rd. It was a twelve mile hike, four thousand feet down and two thousand up. It was the most exhausting hike of my life. We finally made their tents about sundown and we waited for the five sisters to tie up and milk their eighty goats before we celebrated the Eucharist for them. One of their tents was a Chapel with the altar and Blessed Sacrament. They have an indult to self-communicate each day. The Mass was in Latin with readings in French. The tent was barely four foot high, so that by the time Mass was over, I felt I had a broken back. Dinner followed and the first delicacy was fresh goat's milk! I got almost half way through the bowl! But they made delicious whole grain bread and goat's butter is excellent!

We slept on the sand of a "wadi" (dried out river bed) that night and it was a magnificent sky—all night. We were awakened with a predawn breeze that swept down the wadi and reached only a foot or so off the ground. We had Mass at 6:00 a.m. for an American Little Sister who had died in Rome May 6. During the morning we took a long walk down the wadi and met some Tuareg women goatherders and their flock. Continuing further we came to the Tuareg camp and were welcomed by an old man past eighty whom we later learned had welcomed Foucauld here some sixty years ago! At noon we started back for Assekrem but now pushing four donkeys ahead of us! They were in need of water and it took us two hours of walking before we found some higher up in the mountains. Somehow I made it back to Assekrem, God alone knows how. I think I did enough penance for the whole of my life. The next day I was running a fever with chills, the effects of sunstroke on the hike. But a day in bed and the care of Brother Roger had me up the next day.

There are no words to describe those Little Sisters of Jesus in the desert mountains. I can only think of John's Prologue, "And He pitched his tent among them." They are the most beautiful and powerful actualization of the Incarnation I have ever witnessed. They are there simply to show

Christ's love for all men. No one is abandoned or left alone. Each of them is a monument of Jesus' incredible love for men. What would be a veritable martyrdom for us is a way of joy and peace and actually exuberant happiness for them. Such uncompromising Christianity! Literal faith and love alone, lived so intensely and completely that our best pales. I thought to myself, after the desert, can there be anything like a tough assignment?